The Modern RPG IV Language

Reference Summary

The Modern RPGIV Language

Reference Summary

Second Edition - February 1997

Robert Cozzi, Jr.

Publisher: Midrange Computing, Carlsbad, California

First Published April, 1995
Revised and updated February, 1997

Printed in the United States of America

Midrange® is a registered trademark of Robert Cozzi, Jr.
CodeStudio™ is a trademark of Robert Cozzi, Jr.
IBM® is a registered trademark of IBM Corporation.
AS/400™ OS/400™ and 400™ are trademarks of IBM Corporation.

ISBN 1-883884-38-1

Contents

Operation Codes

Abbreviations Used Throughout This Book

Listed in Table 1 are the abbreviations and symbols (referred to here as *tokens*) that are used throughout this book.

Token	Description
[0 or ƀ]	The result of the operation is zero or blank.
[+]	The result of the operation is positive.
[-]	The result of the operation is negative.
[0]	The result of the operation is zero.
[ ]	Brackets denote optional values.
bof	The result of the operation produces a beginning-of-file condition.
eof	The result of the operation produces an end-of-file condition.
[full]	The WRITE operation has filled the subfile specified in Factor 2.
[indn]	Indicator n, where n is 1, 2 or 3.
[mix]	The result of a TESTB operation is some bits on and some off; the result of a TESTN operation is some characters are numeric and some are not.
[num]	The result of the TESTN operation is all numeric.
[other]	The result of the TESTZ operation indicates that the zone of the Result field is neither positive nor negative, it is unknown.
1<2	Factor 1 is less than Factor 2.
1=2	Factor 1 equals Factor 2.
1>2	Factor 1 is greater than Factor 2.
char value	Character value, either literal or variable.
char variable	Character variable—that is, a character field, array, array element, data structure or data structure subfield.
data struct	Data structure name.
dec	Decimal digits (i.e., the number of digits to the right of the decimal point)
n / f	The result of the operation produces a Not Found condition.
num value	Numeric value, either literal or variable.
num blanks	Number of blanks.
num variable	Numeric variable—that is, a numeric field or array element.
plist	Parameter list name.

Table 1: Standard Abbreviations and Symbols

Operation Extender Cross—Reference

The operation extender provides additional operation attributes on various operation codes. For example, to perform rounding with a divide operation, DIV(H) is used. More than one operation extender can be specified. For example, the EVAL operation can specify both half-adjust and the default precision rules as in: EVAL(HM). Table 2 lists the operation extenders and supported opcodes.

Operation Extender	Operation Codes	Meaning and Description
D	CALLB	**Operational Descriptor:** Causes the CALLB operation to include operation descriptor information. This information can be retrieve through a bound call to the CEEDOD API.
H	ADD SUB MULT DIV[1] EVAL Z-ADD Z-SUB SQRT XFOOT	**Half Adjust**: Used to round the result up to the nearest decimal value. This is accomplished by adding $5 * 10^{-(n+1)}$ to the absolute value of the result. Where n = number of decimal positions. For a DEC(5,2) field, the following applies: 1.006 will half adjust to 1.01 -1.006 will half adjust to -1.01
M	EVAL	**Default Precision:** The precision rule for the RPG IV expression is based on the original RPG IV expression rule. This rule uses a large number of decimal positions during intermediate calculations. This operation extender provides the same results as using the EXPROPTS(*MAXDIGITS) keyword. Using this option can cause the results of an expression to be different than the result of the traditional MULT and DIV operations.
N[2]	CHAIN READ READP READE READPE	**Read without locking**: Used when accessing database records from files that are opened for update. This operation extender allows records to be read, but does not place a lock on the record.
N	DEALLOC	**Set Pointer to NULL:** Used when deallocating memory that was allocated by the ALLOC or REALLOC operations.

[1] The half adjust (H) operation extender is valid for independent DIV operations; that is, it cannot be used on DIV operations that are followed by a MVR (move remainder) operation.

[2] In addition to the N operation extender, the UNLOCK operation code can be used to release a locked database record.

Operation Extender	Operation Codes	Meaning and Description
P	CAT MOVE MOVEA MOVEL SUBST XLATE	**Pad Result**: Used to replace the data in the Result field. The P operation extender allows a single operation to replace the contents of the Result field. For character fields, blanks are used to pad the result. For numeric fields, zeros are used.
R	EVAL	**Result-field Precision:** Used when the expression should produce in the same result value as the equivalent MULT and DIV operations. Specify EXPROPTS(*RESDECPOS) on the Header specification, to cause this operation extender to be the default for the entire source file.
T	TEST	**Test Time**: Check the Result field for a valid time.
Z	TEST	**Test Timestamp**: Check the Result field for a valid timestamp.
D	TEST	**Test Date**: Check the Result field for a valid date.

Table 2: Operation Extenders and Supported Opcodes

RPGIV Operation Code Summary Syntax Diagram Legend

Values in square brackets [ ] are optional: For example: [*NOKEY] means *NOKEY is optional. The square brackets can not be included when specifying these values.

The operation code extenders are specified in parentheses in this table, as they are in the language. All operation extenders are optional, but for clarity, they are illustrated here as they are specified in RPGIV (in parentheses) instead of brackets.

Values in lowercase are variable values. For example: *compare value 2* means that a literal or variable (i.e., field) can be specified.

Values in uppercase are constants: for example, *LOCK

The word 'value' generally means any field or literal value can be specified.

The word 'variable' generally means any field, data structure, array, or array element can be specified. For example: *char variable* refers to a field, data structure or array element of type CHARACTER, whereas *num variable* refers to a field of type NUMERIC (such as, packed, binary, or zoned (signed) numeric.)

Table 3 lists the syntax for RPGIV opcodes.

Operation Code Syntax Diagrams

Factor 1	OpCode	Factor 2	Result	Length	Dec	Resulting Ind.		
workstn device ID	ACQ	workstn file name					[error]	
[numeric value]	ADD(H)	numeric value	sum	[size]	[dec]	[+]	[-]	[0]
[base date/time]	ADDDUR	duration:dur code	new date/time					
compare value 1	ANDxx	compare value 2						
	ALLOC	length	pointer				[error]	
[subroutine name]	BEGSR							
	BITOFF	'bit nums to set off'	char variable	[size]				
	BITON	'bit nums to set on'	char variable	[size]				
compare value 1	CABxx	compare value 2	[label]			[1>2]	[1<2]	[1=2]
compare value 1	CAB[3]	compare value 2	[label]			[1>2]	[1<2]	[1=2]
	CALL	program name	[plist]			[error]	[LR]	
	CALLB(D)	proc name or ptr[4]	[plist]			[error]		
[compare value 1]	CASxx	[compare value 2]	subroutine			[1>2]	[1<2]	[1=2]
[operand 1]	CAT(P)	operand 2[:num blanks]	char variable	[size]		[error]		
key value or rec num	CHAIN(N)	record format				n/f	[error]	
key value or rec num	CHAIN(N)	file name	[data struct]			n/f	[error]	
check list	CHECK	base value[:start]	[position(s)]	[size]	[dec]	[error]	[found]	
check list	CHECKR	base value[:start]	[position(s)]	[size]	[dec]	[error]	[found]	
[*NOKEY]	CLEAR	[*ALL]	variable to clear	[size]	[dec]			
	CLOSE	file name				[error]		
	CLOSE	*ALL				[error]		

---

3   If the Result field (label) is not specified, at least one resulting indicator is required.

4   A Procedure Pointer can be a quoted procedure name, a named constant (representing a quoted procedure name), or a pointer variable that has been declared with the PROCPTR keyword specified.

Factor 1	OpCode	Factor 2	Result	Length	Dec	Resulting Ind.		
[boundary]	COMMIT						[error]	
compare value 1	COMP[5]	compare value 2				[1>2]	[1<2]	[1=2]
[descriptive text]	DEBUG	[printer file]	[print value]					
	DEALLOC(N)		pointer				[error]	
*DTAARA	DEFINE	[data area name][6]	assignment	[size]	[dec]			
[key value]	DELETE	file name				[n/f]	[error]	
[key value]	DELETE	record format				[n/f]	[error]	
[numerator]	DIV(H)	denominator	result	[size]	[dec]	[+]	[-]	[0]
[starting value]	DO	[max iterations]	[counter]	[size]	[dec]			
	DOU	expression						
	DOW	expression						
compare value 1	DOUxx	compare value 2						
compare value 1	DOWxx	compare value 2						
[message ID]	DSPLY	[*EXT]	[response]	[size]		[error]		
[message ID]	DSPLY	[message queue]	[response]	[size]		[error]		
[descriptive text]	DUMP							
	ELSE							
	END	[increment]						
	ENDSL							
	ENDDO	[increment][7]						
	ENDIF							
	ENDCAS							
[label]	ENDSR	[return point]						

[5] At least one resulting indicator is required.

[6] If Factor 2 is not specified, the Result field is used as the name of the data structure.

[7] The increment value is valid for END and ENDDO operations associated with a DO operation code.

Factor 1	OpCode	Factor 2	Result	Length	Dec	Resulting Ind.		
	EVAL(H M)	expression						
	EXCEPT	[except output label]						
	EXFMT	record format				[error]		
	EXSR	subroutine						
entity to extract[8]	EXTRCT	date variable:Format	extracted value	[size]	[dec]	[error]		
	FEOD	file name				[error]		
	FORCE	file name						
	GOTO	label						
	IF	expression						
compare value 1	IFxx	compare value 2						
[*LOCK]	IN	data area				[error]		
[*LOCK]	IN	*DTAARA				[error]		
	ITER							
	KFLD		key field					
key list name	KLIST							
	LEAVE							
search pattern	LOOKUP	array(*starting elem*)				[high]	[low]	[equal]
search pattern	LOOKUP	table 1	[table 2]			[high]	[low]	[equal]
	MHHZO	source	char variable	[size]				
	MHLZO	source	char variable	[size]				
	MLHZO	source	char variable	[size]				
	MLLZO	source	char variable	[size]				
[date format][sep] [9]	MOVE(P)	source	target	[size]	[dec]	[+]	[-]	[0 or b]
	MOVEA(P)	source	target	[size]	[dec]	[+]	[-]	[0 or b]

---

[8]   EXTRCT supports: *M (month), *Y (year), *D (date), *W (day of week), *C (century), *MM (minutes), *HH (hour), *SS (second)

[9]   The date format can be any format supported by RPGIV, such as *MDY, *YMD, or *ISO

Factor 1	OpCode	Factor 2	Result	Length	Dec	Resulting Ind.		
[date format][sep]	MOVEL(P)	source	target	[size]	[dec]	[+]	[-]	[0 or b]
[numeric value]	MULT(H)	numeric value	product	[size]	[dec]	[+]	[-]	[0]
	MVR		remainder	[size]	[dec]	[+]	[-]	[0]
workstn device ID	NEXT	workstn file name					[error]	
[occurrence to set to]	OCCUR	data structure	[occurrence]	[size]	[dec]		[error]	
	OPEN	file name					[error]	
compare value 1	ORxx	compare value 2						
	OTHER							
[*LOCK]	OUT	data area					[error]	
[*LOCK]	OUT	*DTAARA					[error]	
[input value]	PARM	[output value]	parameter	[size]	[dec]			
parameter list name	PLIST							
[workstn device ID]	POST	workstn file name[10]	[infds]				[error]	
	REALLOC	length	pointer				[error[	
	READ(N)	record format					[error]	eof
	READ(N)	file name	[data struct]				[error]	eof
	READC	subfile record format					[error]	eof
[key value]	READE(N)	record format					[error]	eof
[key value]	READE(N)	file name	[data struct]				[error]	eof
	READP(N)	record format					[error]	bof
	READP(N)	file name	[data struct]				[error]	bof
[key value]	READPE(N)	record format					[error]	bof
[key value]	READPE(N)	file name	[data struct]				[error]	bof
workstn device ID	REL	workstn file name					[error]	
[*NOKEY]	RESET	[*ALL]	variable to reset	[size]	[dec]			

---

[10]   Factor 2 is optional when a workstation device file's INFDS data structure name is specified for the Result field.

Factor 1	OpCode	Factor 2	Result	Length	Dec	Resulting Ind.		
	RETURN	expression to return						
	ROLBK					[error]		
search pattern[:length]	SCAN	search var[:start]	[position(s)][11]	[size]	[dec]	[error]	[found]	
search pattern[:length]	SCANR	search var[:start]	[position(s)]	[size]	[dec]	[error]	[found]	
	SELECT							
key value	SETGT	file name				[n/f]	[error]	
key value	SETGT	record format				[n/f]	[error]	
key value	SETLL	file name				[n/f]	[error]	[found]
key value	SETLL	record format				[n/f]	[error]	[found]
	SETOFF					[ind1]	[ind2]	[ind3]
	SETON					[ind1]	[ind2]	[ind3]
	SHUTDN					yes		
	SORTA	array						
	SQRT(H)	numeric value	square root	[size]	[dec]			
[numeric value]	SUB(H)	numeric value	difference	[size]	[dec]	[+]	[-]	[0]
[date / time]	SUBDUR	duration:dur code	date / time			[error]		
date / time	SUBDUR	date / time	duration:dur code	[size]	[dec]	[error]		
[length of source]	SUBST(P)	source var[:start]	char variable	[size]		[error]		
label	TAG							
format to test	TEST(D, T, Z)		date / time variable			[error]		
	TESTB	'bit numbers to test'	char variable	[size]		[xor]	[mix]	[equal]
	TESTN		char variable	[size]		[num]	[mix]	[blank]
	TESTZ		char variable	[size]		[+]	[-]	[other]
	TIME		num variable	[size]	[dec]			

---

[11]   If the Result field is omitted, resulting indicator 3 is required.

Factor 1	OpCode	Factor 2	Result	Length	Dec	Resulting Ind.		
	UNLOCK	data area | *DTAARA				[error]		
	UNLOCK	file name				[error]		
	UPDATE	record format				[error]		
	UPDATE	file name	[data struct]			[error]		
	WHEN	expression						
compare value 1	WHENxx	compare value 2						
	WRITE	record format				[error]	[full][12]	
	WRITE	file name	[data struct]			[error]		
	XFOOT(H)	numeric array	sum of array	[size]	[dec]	[+]	[-]	[0]
from value : to value	XLATE(P)	source[:start]	char variable	[size]		[error]		
	Z-ADD(H)	numeric value	num variable	[size]	[dec]	[+]	[-]	[0]
	Z-SUB(H)	numeric value	num variable	[size[	[dec]	[+]	[-]	[0]

Table 3: RPGIV OpCode Syntax Diagram

---

[12]   Resulting indicator 2 [full] is valid only for WRITE operations to a WORKSTN subfile detail record format.

Language Extents

Language Extents

Feature	RPGIV Extension
AN/OR (columns 7-8 of Calc Spec)	No limit
Array elements	32,767
Arrays and tables	No limit
Compile-time array or table length	100 positions
Data structure length (named)	32,767
Data structure length (unnamed)	9,999,999 positions
Data structure occurrences	32,767
Edit word length	115 positions
Field length	Char: 32,767 positions; Numeric: (30 30) positions
Field name	14 or 4096 characters[13]
Files per program	No limit
File key length (program described)	Limited to file length
File key length (externally described)	Limited to file length
Hexadecimal literal values	1024 characters
Lines per page (program described)	2 to 255 lines
Lines per page (externally described)	1 to 255 lines
Spacing before/after print line	0 to 255 lines
Skipping to a specific print line	1 to 255
Matched fields (combined length)	256 positions
Named constants	Char: 1,024 positions; Numeric: (30 30) positions
Nested IF, DOxxx, SELECT groups	100 levels
Nested /COPY directives	1 minimum, 2048 maximum, 32 is the default
Parameters	255 Dynamic; 399 Bound Call
Primary files	1 per program
Printer files (program described)	8 per program
Printer files (externally described)	No limit
Record address files (ADDROUT)	1 per program
Record format length	32,767 positions
Subroutines	32,767 per module
Subprocedures	No limit

Table 4: RPGIV Language Extents

---

[13] Depending on the version of RPG IV, the maximum length of a field name is either 10 characters or 4096 characters. When the maximum length is 4096, the practical length is 14 characters.

Reserved Words

Reserved Words Overview

There are a number of reserved words in RPG. These reserved words are referred to as special names. All special names begin with a unique symbol (such as an asterisk or percent sign). The exceptions to this are the UDATE, UDAY, UMONTH and UYEAR fields. The PAGE field, however, while technically a reserved word, can be declared with an alternative length and manipulated like any other field.

Note for date and time formatting codes, see *Date and Time Data Types* beginning on page 57.

There are many different classifications of reserved words in RPG, including:

1. *Reserved Fields*: Special field names containing a specific value. Typically, these values can be changed at runtime.

2. *Figurative Constants*: Special field names whose value is constant or is established at pre-runtime. The content of these fields cannot be changed.

3. *Control Values*: Special values that control operation code function or Output specification results.

4. *Routines*: Special routines within the RPG cycle.

5. *Built-in Functions*: Special routines that provide addition string, math, and expression functions.

These types of reserved words are defined in the charts on the pages that follow.

Reserved Words

Reserved Field	Description
NOT	Used in expressions to reverse the result of the expression. Note, the word NOT is the only reserved word in RPG. No other value (including fields) can be named NOT.
PAGE	Page number. This 4-digit numeric field is used as a page counter. It is incremented each time it is output. You can change the defined length of this field by simply declaring it in your program with another length.
PAGEn	Additional page counters. These 4-digit numeric fields are used as additional page counters. PAGEn, where n can be 1 to 7, offers 7 additional page counters. You can change the defined length of these fields by simply declaring it in your program with another length.
UDATE	Session date. This 6-digit numeric field is initialized to the run-date when the program is started. The format of this date is based on the format specified in the Header specification for the program.
UDAY	Session day. This 2-digit numeric field contains the day of the month.
UMONTH	Session month. This 2-digit numeric field contains the month.
UYEAR	Session year. This 2-digit numeric field contains the year.
*DATE	Used to retrieve the current date. This date value represents the date with 8 positions. For example, if the date format is *MDY, *DATE will contain mmddccyy, where cc=century; yy=year; mm=month; dd=day. Unlike UDATE, *DATE cannot be modified at program runtime. The format of this date is based on the format specified in the Header specification for the program
*MONTH	Used to retrieve the current month. This date value represents the month in mm format. Where mm=month.
*YEAR	Used to retrieve the current century and year. This date value represents the year in ccyy format, where cc=century; yy=year.
*DAY	Used to retrieve the current day. This date value represents the day of the month in dd format, where dd=day of the month.

Table 5: Reserved Words

Figurative Constants

Figurative constants can be used with most operation codes and anywhere an expression is allowed. Figurative constants can be used on the Definition and Calculation specifications.

Figurative Value	Description
*ALL'...'	Repeating pattern. Automatically adjusts to the size of the corresponding field that it is being compared with or moved to. For example: *ALL'abcd' moves 'abcdabcd' etc. to the Result field for the length of the Result field.
*ALLX'...'	Repeating hexadecimal pattern. Automatically adjusts to the size of the corresponding field that it is being compared with or moved to. For example: *ALLX'00' moves binary zeros to the Result field for the length of the Result field.
*ALLG'so...si'	Repeating graphic character set (DBCS) pattern. Automatically adjusts to the size of the corresponding DBCS field.
*BLANK *BLANKS	Blanks. Automatically adjusts to the size of corresponding field that it is being compared with or moved to them.
*END	Use the special value *END in Factor 1 of the SETLL operation to position the file *cursor* to the end of the file.
*HIVAL	Represents the highest possible value for the corresponding data type. It can be compared with or moved to a field.
*LOVAL	Represents the lowest possible value for the corresponding data type. It can be compared with or moved into a field.
*NULL	Use to set or compare pointer data types to "no value". Currently, RPG supports *NULL with the pointer data type.
*OFF	Logical off ('0'). Functionally similar to *ALL'0'. Typically, *OFF is used with the IFxx and MOVE operations to test or set the status of an indicator.
*ON	Logical on ('1'). Functionally similar to *ALL'1'. Typically, *ON is used with the IFxx and MOVE operations to test or set the status of an indicator.
*OMIT	Use this value on parameters that are being skipped during a bound call (i.e., CALLB or CALLP) operation.
*START	Use the special value *START in Factor 1 of the SETLL operation to position to the beginning of the file.
*ZERO *ZEROS	Used to represent a repeating pattern of zeros. Can be used with any data type, except *pointer, date, time,* and *timestamp* variables.
*ASTFILL	Used with the %EDITC built-in function to indicate that the edited value is to be padded on the left-side with leading asterisks.
*CURSYM	Used with the %EDITC built-in function to indicate that the currency symbol is to be inserted into the edited value.

Table 6: Figurative Constants

Operation Code Parameter Values

Control Value	Operation Codes	Description
*ENTRY	PLIST	The *ENTRY parameter list identifies the parameter list used to pass parameters into and return parameters from the program.
*INZSR	BEGSR	The *INZSR subroutine, if specified in the program, is called by the RPG cycle before 1P output.
*TERMSR	BEGSR	The *TERMSR subroutine, if specified, is called by RPG when the program is ending—after all other processing is competed.
*LIKE	DEFINE	The *LIKE DEFINE operation code is used to define a new field, based on the attributes of another field. The types of fields that can be defined with *LIKE DEFINE are character and packed decimal.
*LOCK	IN	The *LOCK IN operation code is used to read a data area, then place an object-lock on that data area.
	OUT	The *LOCK OUT operation code is used to write a data area and retain the object-lock.
*LDA	DEFINE	The *DTAARA DEFINE *LDA operation code is used to assign a variable to receive the contents of the local data area.
*PDA	DEFINE	The *DTAARA DEFINE *PDA operation code is used to assign a variable to receive the program initialization parameters.
*DTAARA	DEFINE	The *DTAARA DEFINE operation code is used to declare the entry in Factor 2 as a data area. An optional field name can be specified in the Result field. If Factor 2 is not specified, the field name in the Result field is used as the data area name.
	IN	The IN *DTAARA operation code is used to read all data areas defined in the program. If *LOCK IN *DTAARA is specified, all data areas defined in the program are read and an object-lock is placed on each one.
	OUT	The OUT *DTAARA operation is used to write (i.e., output) all data areas defined in the program. If *LOCK OUT *DTAARA is specified, all data areas are written and any object-locks are retained.
*PSSR	BEGSR	The *PSSR subroutine, if specified in the program, is called by the RPG exception/error handling routine whenever an unmonitored error occurs.

Table 7: Control Values Used in Calculation Specifications

Output Control Values

Control Field	Description
*ALL	Output all fields. This control field causes all fields from an externally defined file to be output. It is used on Output specifications controlled by an EXCEPT operation code.
*PLACE	Asterisk-Place. This control field replicates Output specifications, within the specific output line up to the position of the *PLACE. The replicated output is positioned at the end position specified for the *PLACE. *PLACE is (or more accurately, "was") used in label printing programs to print 2-, 3-, and 4-up labels. It was created primarily to automate printed output from 80-column card-based programs. It is virtually worthless today considering the on-line source editors available.

Table 8: Control Fields Used in Output Specifications

Subroutine Return Points

Routine	Description
*CANCL	Cancel the program.
*DETC	Return to detail-time calculations.
*DETL	Return to detail-time lines (i.e., detail output).
*GETIN	Return to the next "get in" cycle.
*NEXT	Return to the statement following the one in which the error occurred.
*OFL	Return to the overflow output-time portion of the cycle.
*TOTC	Return to total-time calculations.
*TOTL	Return to total-time lines (i.e., total-time output).
Blanks	If the *PSSR or INFSR subroutines were called by the EXSR or CASxx operation, control returns to the statement following the EXSR or CASxx operation. If the RPG exception/error handler called the subroutine, the following applies: If the error status code is 1121 to 1126, control returns to the operation where the error occurred. Any other error status code causes an exception to be issued and the requester is notified (i.e., a message is sent to the user).

Table 9: *PSSR and INFSR Subroutine Return Points

Built-In Functions

Built-In Functions List

Built-in functions can be used with the IF, DOW, DOU, EVAL, CALLP, RETURN, and WHEN operations. These operation codes support the extended Factor 2 Calculation specification. Built-in functions cannot be used with traditional opcodes, such as DO, and CASEQ. In addition, many built-in functions can be used in the function / keyword area of the Definition (D) specification. They cannot, however, be used in the function / keyword area of the Header or File Description specifications.

Function	Description
%SUBST	Substring a character string.
%SIZE	Return the declared size of a field.
%ELEM	Return the number of declared elements in an array.
%TRIM	Trim trailing and leading blanks.
%TRIML	Trim leading blanks.
%TRIMR	Trim trailing blanks.
%PARMS	Return the number of parameters passed into the program/procedure.
%ADDR	Return the address of a variable to a pointer variable.
%PADDR	Return the procedure address to a procedure pointer variable.

All built-in functions have the following syntax:

```
%funct( arg1 : arg2 : ... argn )
```

Built-in functions must begin with a percent sign followed by the built-in function name, followed by parentheses. Enclosed in the parentheses are one or more parameters, which are referred to as *arguments*. These arguments can be any valid literal, field, expression, or another built-in function. When more than one argument is specified, they are separated by the colon (:) symbol. Spaces are not significant to built-in functions or expressions.

Built-In Function Syntax

The following table illustrates the syntax for each RPG built-in function. Italicized words are variable and / or expressions, values enclosed in brackets are optional arguments.

Return Value	Function Syntax
char string	%SUBST(*variable* : *starting-position* [: *length*])
decl length of variable	%SIZE(*variable* [:*ALL*])
number of elements	%ELEM(*array* | *data-structure*)
char string	%TRIM(*character-variable*)
char string	%TRIML(*character-variable*)
char string	%TRIMR(*character-variable*)
number of parameters passed in	%PARMS()
pointer to variable	%ADDR(*variable*)
procedure pointer	%PADDR('*procedure-name*')

An example use of a built-in function follows:

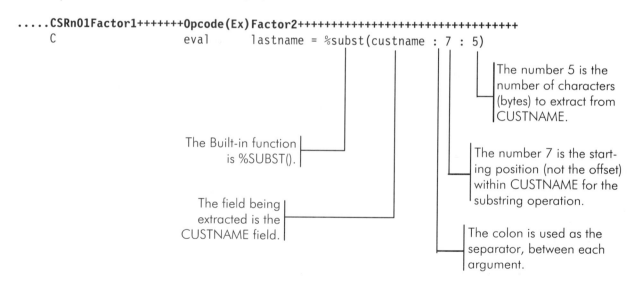

```
.....CSRn01Factor1+++++++Opcode(Ex)Factor2++++++++++++++++++++++++++++++++++
     C                   eval      lastname = %subst(custname : 7 : 5)
```

The number 5 is the number of characters (bytes) to extract from CUSTNAME.

The Built-in function is %SUBST().

The number 7 is the starting position (not the offset) within CUSTNAME for the substring operation.

The field being extracted is the CUSTNAME field.

The colon is used as the separator, between each argument.

%ADDR() Substring Function

This function returns the memory location assigned to a variable. This memory location is known as the variable's *address*.

Syntax Diagram

$$pointer\text{-}to\text{-}variable = \%ADDR(\ variable\ )$$

You can specify any variable, data structure, subfield, array, or array element on the %ADDR() function.

Use this function to return the address of a variable when you are using pointers. For example, if you have a pointer variable named MYPOINTER, you can store the address of another variable in it by using the %ADDR() function as follows:

```
.....DName++++++++++EUDSFrom+++To/Len+TDc.Functions+++++++++++++++++++++++++++++++
0001 *   Stand-alone field is: COMP_DESC  Type is Char(35)
0002 D Comp_Desc       S              35A
0003
0004 *   Stand-alone field is: MYPOINTER  Type is pointer
0005 D myPointer       S               *   INZ(%ADDR(Comp_Desc))
```

In this example, the stand-alone field named COMP_DESC is defined as a 35-position character field (line 2). This variable's address in memory is allocated at program runtime.

On line 5, the variable named MYPOINTER is declared. Its data type is an asterisk (*). This declares it to be of type *pointer*. Pointers contain the addresses of other variables.

In the Function area of line 5, the INZ() keyword (initial value) is used to initialize the MYPOINTER variable to the address (memory location) of the COMP_DESC field.

Another way to assign addresses with the %ADDR() built-in function is with the EVAL operation, as follows:

```
.....CSRn01Factor1+++++++Opcode(E)+Factor2+++++++++++++++++++++++++++++++++++++++++
     C                   Eval      myPointer = %ADDR( Comp_Desc )
```

%ELEM() Number of Elements Function

This function returns the number of elements declared for an array, table, or the number of occurrences of a multiple occurrence data structure.

Syntax Diagram

> `number-of-elements = %ELEM( array )`
>
> `number-of-occurrences = %ELEM( data-structure )`

Specify the name of an array, table, or multiple occurrence data structure on the %ELEM() function. If an array name is specified, optionally, specify the dimension of the array whose element count is to be returned.

Use this function in place of "hard coding" a reference to the number of elements of an array or data structure. Use the resulting value to control code, such as DO loops and substring operations. For example:

```
.....DName++++++++++EUDSFrom+++To/Len+TDc.Functions++++++++++++++++++++++++++
0001 D  State            S             2A   DIM(50)

.....CsrN01Factor1+++++++Opcode(E)+Factor2++++++++++++++++++++++++++++++++++++
0002  * The following code, extracts the element count (50) of the STATE array
0003 C                   Eval      Limit = %ELEM(State)

.....C*ON01Factor1+++++++Opcode(E)+Factor2+++++++Result++++++++Len++D+HiLoEq
0004 C                   DO        Limit        nIndex           3 0
0005 C                   MOVEL     State(nIndex) WhereEver
0006 C* ....... other code goes here.......
0007 C                   enddo
```

%PADDR() Procedure Address

This function returns the address assigned to a procedure. A procedure is similar to a subroutine, except a procedure can be called by other programs. Procedures are called through a *procedure pointer* variable that contains the address of the procedure.

Syntax Diagram

$$pointer\text{-}to\text{-}procedure = \%PADDR(\ 'quoted\text{-}literal'\ )$$

Specify a quoted character string, a hexadecimal value, or a named constant on the %PADDR() function.

Procedure addresses are resolved when program modules are linked together ("bound"). Therefore, the compiler must be able to resolve procedure names during the link phase. This is in contrast to the dynamic CALL operation that resolves program addresses at runtime.

```
.....DName++++++++++EUDSFrom+++To/Len+TDc.Functions++++++++++++++++++++++++++++
0001  *   Declare a Procedure Pointer
0002 D getcursor      S             *       procptr                      | Procedure pointer
0003 D row            S            10I 0                          ◄──────| variable is declared
0004 D column         S            10I 0                                 | on the D spec.
0005
.....CsrN01Factor1+++++++Opcode(E)+Factor2++++++++++++++++++++++++++++++++++++++
0006  *   Retrieve the procedure pointer to a DSM API
0007 C                    Eval      getcursor = %PADDR('QsnGetCsrAdr')
0008
.....CsrN01Factor1+++++++Opcode(E)+Factor2+++++++Result++++++++Len++D+HiLoEq
0009  * Call the DSM API using a procedure pointer variable
0010 C                    CALLB     getcursor
0011 C                    parm                   row
0012 C                    parm                   column
```

%PARMS - Get Number of Parameters Passed to Program/Procedure

This function returns the number of parameters passed to the program or ILE procedure. The value returned here, is the same value the appears in the *PARMS locations of the Program Status Data Structure (PSDS).

Syntax Diagram

numeric-return-variable = %PARMS

Example

```
.....DName++++++++++EUDSFrom+++To/Len+TDc.Functions++++++++++++++++++++++++++++
0001 D nParms          S              4S 0 INZ(0)
0002 D i               S              3S 0

.....CSRn01..............OpCode(ex)Extended-factor2++++++++++++++++++++++++++++++
.....CSRn01Factor1+++++++Opcode(E)+Factor2+++++++Result++++++++Len++D+HiLoEq
      * Copy %parms to numeric variable
0003 C                   Eval      nParms = %parms
0004 C                   Do        nParms           I
      * Test %PARMS() for specific value
0005 C                   Select
0006 C                   When      %parms = 1
0007 C                   exsr      OneParm
0008 C                   When      %parms = 2
0009 C                   exsr      TwoParms
0010 C                   When      %parms = 3
0011 C                   exsr      ThreeParms
0012 C                   other
0013 C                   exsr      TooMany
0014 C                   endsl
0015 C                   enddo
```

%SIZE - Get Bytes Used to Store Variable

This function returns the size (in bytes) of a variable or literal value. For character and signed numeric values, the value returned is also the length of the field. For packed numeric fields, the value returned is caculated using the packing algorithm. That is (length + 1) / 2 rounded to the down to the nearest whole number. So a 7-position packed field returns a %SIZE() value of 4.

Syntax Diagram

$$numeric\text{-}return\text{-}value = \%SIZE(\ value\ [\ :\ *ALL\ ]\ )$$

For a field or named constant, the number of bytes returned is the declared length of the field or implied length of the named constant. For tables and arrays, or multiple occurrence data structures, the length of a single element or occurrence is returned. If the size of an entire array, table, or data structure is desired, use the *ALL optional parameter.

```
.....DName++++++++++EUDSFrom+++To/Len+TDc.Functions+++++++++++++++++++++++++++++
0001 D Arr_Size       S               7p 0 INZ(0)
0003 D Comp_Name       S              35A
0004  * Declare an array using the built-in function to determine its elements
0005 D DATA            S               1A   DIM( %SIZE(COMP_NAME) )
0006
.....CSRn01.............OpCode(ex)Extended-factor2++++++++++++++++++++++++++++++++
0007  * Extract the size of all the elements in the DATA array
0008 C                  Eval      Arr_Size = %size( DATA : *ALL )
```

%SUBST() Substring a Value

This function (a) returns a portion of a value or variable, and (b) identifies a target of a variable to be assigned a value (copied to) using the EVAL operation code.

Syntax Diagram

```
return-value = %SUBST( value : start [ : length ] )

%SUBST( value : start [ : length ] )  = value-to-assign
```

The %SUBST() function accepts three parameters:

1. The base value to be "substringed"
2. The starting position within the base value
3. The number of bytes, (including the starting position) to be included (optional)

If the 3rd parameter is omitted, the default is to use the length from the starting position to the end of the base value. The first parameter must a variable or a character string expression. The second and third parameters can be a variable or a numeric expression.

The %SUBST() function is the only built-in function that can be specified on either size of the assignment symbol of the EVAL operation code. When %SUBST() is being used to assign a value to a portion of another value (i.e., on the left side of the equal sign), then the first parameter must be a variable.

%TRIM(), %TRIML(), %TRIMR() Trim Leading and/or Trailing Blanks

This function analyzes a string value and returns a string with its leading and / or trailing blank characters removed. Typically these functions are used to concatenate a set of character string values together.

%TRIML()	Removes leading blank characters.
%TRIMR()	Removes trailing blank characters.
%TRIM()	Removes both leading and trailing blank characters.

Syntax Diagram

$$character\text{-}return\text{-}value = \%TRIMx(\ value\ )$$

The value returned is a character string. It can be assigned to a variable, or used in an expression. The *value* parameter must be a character value, including an expression, quoted character string, or character variable.

```
.....CSRn01Factor1+++++++Opcode(E)+Factor2+++++++Result++++++++Len++D+HiLoEq
0001 C                   MOVE      *BLANKS     NAME              25
0002 C                   MOVE(p)   'Bob'       FIRST             20
0003 C                   MOVE(p)   'Cozzi'     LAST              20

.....CSRn01..............OpCode(ex)Extended-factor2++++++++++++++++++++++++++++
0004 C                   EVAL      Name = %TRIM(First) + ' ' + %TRIML(Last)
0005
0006 C*                            1...v....1....v....2....v
0007 C*  The result field NAME = 'Bob Cozzi              '
```

32

Keyword Functions

Keyword Functions Syntax

Keywords can be used on the Header, File Description, and Definition specification. They are used for various purposes, such as extending the attributes of fields, specifying file controls, and setting up program-wide (global) attributes.

Many keywords accept parameters, some parameters are optional, some are required. All parameter values are specified within parentheses. If more than one value is required for a keyword, the subsequent values are separated by a colon, for example:

```
OVERLAY( custnum : 7)
```

In the list of keywords below, optional parameters are enclosed in square brackets [ ]. These brackets are not part of the parameter value, and should not be specified. For example:

```
OVERLAY( subfield [ : position ] )
```

Note the colon is enclosed in the square brackets. This indicates that when the optional parameter is specified, the colon must also appear as the delimiter.

Header Specification Keywords

Keyword	Parameters	Description
ATLSEQ	*NONE *SRC *EXT	Alternate collating sequence. Identifies where the collating sequence is specified. A value of *SRC or just the keyword, indicates it is specified near the end of the source program, with the **ALTSEQ identifier. The *EXT indicates the collating sequence is specified when the program is compiled.
COPYNEST	1 to 2048 32	Specifies the number of /COPY nesting levels that are accepted by the compiler. The default is 32, however, up to 2048 nesting levels are allowed by the RPG IV compiler.
COPYRIGHT	'copyright info.'	Specify up to 256 characters that represent the copyright notice. This notice is stored within the compiled program.
CURSYM	'symbol'	Any quoted character or symbol, except the following, can be specified: *, 0, , (comma), . (period), -, C, R, or a blank.
DATEDIT	format [separator]	Sets the default format for numeric fields that are edited with the Y edit code. Valid entries are: *MDY, *YMD, and *DMY. The separator can be any separator character and defaults to the slash (/).
DATFMT	format [separator]	Specifies the default format to be used for date fields and date literals within the program. If this keyword is not specified, the *ISO format (ccyy-mm-dd) is used. The separator can be any valid separator character. See Date Formats on page 59 for more information.
DEBUG	*NO *YES	Controls output of the DUMP operation code.
DECEDIT	'symbol'	Controls the symbol used to edit numeric values in the program. Valid entries are: '.' Decimal point is the period with zeros suppressed (.123) ',' Decimal point is the comma with zeros suppressed (,123) '0.' Decimal point is the period (0.123) '0,' Decimal point is the comma (0,123)
DFTNAME	program name	The default name for the program.
EXPROPTS	*MAXDIGITS	Math preformed in an expression will use temporary result fields with a large number of decimal positions. This often produces results that are different from similar MULT and DIV operations.
	*RESDECPOS	Math performed in an expression will use temporary result fields with the same number of decimal positions as the target result field. This can sometimes lead to results that are different from similar MULT and DIV operations.
FORMSALIGN	*NO *YES	This option causes a message to be sent to the system operator immediately after the first line of output is printed.

Keyword	Parameters	Description
FTRANS	*NONE *SRC	Identifies whether or not file translation will occur. The translation table must be specified near the bottom of the source program with the **FTRANS identifier.
TIMFMT	format [*separator*]	Specifies the default format and separator for *time fields* and *time literals* used in the program. If this keyword is not specified, *ISO format (hh.mm.ss 24 hour clock) is used.

Table 10: Header Specification Keywords

File Description Specification Keyword Functions

The RPG File Description specification supports File Continuation Keywords. These keywords are specified in columns 44 to 80 of the File Description specification.

Several File Continuation keywords support parameter options. These parameters are specified in parentheses immediately following the keyword name. (See File Description Specification Keyword Functions starting on page 38.)

File Continuation keywords provide many additional control features, including the ability to:

- Rename, include, and omit specific formats from an externally defined file.
- Assign a record number field to a subfile detail record format.
- Assign a field to control the starting line number of a WORKSTN device file.
- Assign an information data structure to a specific file.
- Assign a print-control data structure to a PRINTER device file.

Several samples of the File Continuation keywords are illustrated in Table 11.

```
*...v....1....v....2....v....3....v....4....v....5....v....6....v....7....v....8
.....FFilename++IPEASFRlen+LKlen+AIDevice+.Functions+++++++++++++++++++++++++++++
0001 FDISPLAY   CF                    WORKSTN INFDS(WSDS) IGNORE(DONTNEED)
0002 F                                        RENAME(REALNAME : NEWNAME)
0003 F                                        SFILE(sfldetail : rrn)
0004 F                                        SLN(line)
0005
0006 FCUSTMAST  IF                    DISK    INFDS(CUSTDS)
0007 F                                        RENAME(CUSTREC : custmast)
0008
0009 FQPRINT    O    F  132           PRINTER PRTCTL(PRTCTL : *COMPAT)
```

Table 11: Sample File Continuation Keyword Usage

File Continuation Keywords

Keyword	Parameter	Description
COMMIT	*Indicator variable*	This file is under commitment control. COMMIT and ROLLBACK operation codes can be used to control changes made to the file.

BLOCK	*YES	Record blocking occurs if the following conditions are met:
		
		1. The file is program-described or, if externally described, it has only one record format.
		2. The keyword RECNO is not used in the file-description specification.
		3. One of the following is true:
		
		  A. The file is an output file.
		  B. If the file is a combined file and it is an array or table.
		  C. The file is an input-only file; it is not a record-address file or processed by a record-address file; and none of the following operations are used in the file: READE, READPE and READP.

	*NO	No record blocking occurs.
DATFMT	date fmt [separator]	Key field format; used when the key of the database file is a date data type. The RPG syntax for date and date separator is as follows: *MDY/ where *MDY is the date format / is the separator.
DEVID	*Char field*	A 10-character field name that contains the WORKSTN device name for read operations and from write operations to the device.
EXTIND	External Indicator	The corresponding file is opened at start up time only when the external indicator is on. Valid indicators are: *INU1 through *INU8
FORMLEN	forms length	Controls the number of lines that can be sent to a PRINTER output file before a new page is detected.
FORMOFL	overflow line number	Identifies the overflow line for the PRINTER output device. When this is printed on or passed, the indicator specified by the OFLIND() keyword is set on by RPG.
IGNORE	format1 : format2...	The record format names are not included in the program and cannot be referenced.
INCLUDE	format1 : format2...	Only the record format names specified as parameters of this keyword are included in the program, all other record formats are not accessible, unless specified on an SFILE() or another INCLUDE() keyword.
INFDS	Data structure	The name of the file information data structure. The INFDS contains information about the file and the input/output operations associated with it.

Keyword	Parameter	Description
INFSR	Subroutine *PSSR	The name of the file exception/error handling subroutine that will be evoked, automatically, when an unmonitored exception/error occurs on this file. If *PSSR is specified and no user-written *PSSR subroutine exists, the default RPG exception/error handling routine is called. If a custom *PSSR subroutine exists in the program, it is called.
KEYLOC	Key position	The position within the database file that contains the first character for the keyfields. This keyword is ignored by RPG.
MAXDEV	*ONLY *FILE	The maximum number of WORKSTN devices (display or ICF) that can be acquired by this program. Use this keyword to perform workstation time-out via the DDS INVITE keyword.
OFLIND	Overflow Indicator	Assigns an indicator to a file of type PRINTER. This indicator is set on by RPG when the print line specified by the FORMOFL() keyword is printed on.
PASS	*NOIND	Avoids passing indicators to the workstation device file. This keyword applies only to program described input WORKSTN device files.
PGMNAME	special device driver	The name of the program to use as the input/output device driver for the SPECIAL device file.
PLIST	PLIST name	The name of a named parameter list (named PLIST) to be used by the SPECIAL device file I/O routine. The named PLIST is passed (in addition to the parameter list that follows) to the program specified as the SPECIAL device file I/O routine. The parameters from the named PLIST are added to the following parameter list: OPCODE CHAR(1) /* Operation */ O = Open the file C = Close the file R = Read from the file W = Write to the file D = Delete the current record U = Update the current record RTNCOD CHAR(1) /* Return code */ 0 = Normal completion 1 = End or Beginning of file 2 = Exception/error occurred ERRCOD ZONED(5,0) /* Error code */ Returned to the *RECORD subfield of the INFDS data structure for the file.

Keyword	Parameter	Description
PLIST *cont.*		BUFFER CHAR(*) /* Data from or for the record */ The data for the record is placed into this parameter and returned to the input record format of the SPECIAL device file. The actual length of this parameter, as passed to the program, is equal to the file length specified for the SPECIAL device file. This parameter list is automatically generated by RPG in the program that contains the SPECIAL device file. In the program being used as the SPECIAL device file's I/O routine, however, this parameter list must be specified.
PREFIX	prefix [: *replace size*]	For Externally Described files, the prefix is used to automatically rename all fields in the file. The prefix is appended to the front of the field name of each field in the record format. The prefix is not enclosed in quotes. For example: PREFIX(CM) causes the fields: ACTNO, CUSTNM, and CUSTAD to be renamed to: CMACTNO, CMCUSTNM, and CMCUSTAD and PREFIX(CM_)causes those same fields to be renamed to: CM_ACTNO, CM_CUSTNM, and CM_CUSTAD The optional *Replacement Size* can be used to trim off the first *n* characters from field names before applying the prefix. For example: PREFIX(CST_ : 2) causes the field named CMNAME to be renamed to: CST_NAME, and a field named ACTNO is renamed to: CST_TNO. Use this option when field names have already had a prefix used in their original name. The total length of the renamed field name cannot exceed the maximum length for an RPGIV field name. The Input specification restricts names to 14 positions, including a prefix.

PRTCTL	*DS name* [: *COMPAT]	Printer device file control data structure. The data structure must be at least 15 positions in length unless *COMPAT is specified, in which case the data structure must be at least 9 positions. The following is the default PRTCTL data structure format:
		<pre>dDSName.........DS... Length+TDc.Function++
		dPRTCTL DS
		d SpaceBefor 3S 0
		d SpaceAfter 3S 0
		d SkipBefore 3S 0
		d SkipAfter 3S 0
		d CurLine 3S 0</pre>

Keyword	Parameter	Description

PRTCTL *cont.*		The following is the PRTCTL data structure format when *COMPAT is specified:
		
		`dDSName.........DS...       Length+TDc.Function++`
		`dPRTCTL         DS`
		`d SpaceBefor                  1A`
		`d SpaceAfter                  1A`
		`d SkipBefore                  2A`
		`d SkipAfter                   2A`
		`d CurLine                     3S 0`
		
		Note: CURLIN field is the line number on the current page.

RAFDATA	file name	Record address file. The name of a database file that contains the sort order for the database file being declared. The file specified here is normally referred to as an ADDROUT file.
RECNO	Numeric field	Record number of the record just accessed by an OPEN or an I/O operation is placed into this field. If the file uses blocking (normally associated with sequential processing and specified outside the program), the value in this field is often invalid.
RENAME	old name : new name	Change the name of an externally described file record format.
SAVEDS	Data structure	Save data structure name. The name of a data structure that RPG will save before output, and then restore before input of an acquired device is read or written. The SAVDS keyword can be used by RPGII MRT programs that run in the AS/400 S/36 environment and AS/400 multiple device files.
SAVEIND	Indicator to save	The number of indicators to save and restore for each I/O operation.
SAVIND	01 to 99	The number of indicators that must be saved for each for input/output operations to an attached device file.
SFILE	Format name : relno	Subfile detail record format. This keyword serves two functions: (1) It defines a record format as a subfile detail record. (2) It associates a numeric field with the subfile. The numeric field is used as the subfile relative record number. The *relno* field is the name the field that will be used as the subfile's relative record number. You set the value in this field for CHAIN and WRITE operations to the subfile. RPG sets this field when you perform a READC (read changed subfile record) or a CHAIN (random get) operation.
SLN	Numeric field	Variable starting line number field. The field that is used to control the variable starting line number for the WORKSTN (display) device file formats. To use SLN(), the WORKSTN (display) device file must contain the SLNO(*VAR) keyword in its DDS.

Keyword	Parameter	Description
TIMFMT	time format [sep]	Key field format. Used when the data type for the key of a program described database file is TIME. See Table 23 on page 60 for a list of supported TIME formats.
USROPN		The file being declared is not automatically opened by RPG when the program is started. The file can be opened by an OPEN operation in this program, or by another program or procedure.

Table 12: File Continuation Keywords

Definition Specification Keywords

Keyword	Parameters	Description
ALIGN		The ALIGN keyword is used to align data structure subfields for better performance. Alignment is done based on the size of the subfield, it's type, and location within the data structure subfield. When ALIGN is specified the following alignment occurs when necessary: 2-byte integer subfields are aligned on a 2-byte boundary. 4-byte integer and floating point subfields are aligned on a 4-byte boundary. 8-byte floating-point subfields are aligned on an 8-byte boundary. Pointer subfields are aligned on a 16-byte boundary. ALIGN is not allowed for the file information data structure (INFDS) or the program status data structure (PSDS).
ALT	array name	The name of an alternate table or array name.
ALTSEQ	*NONE	The ALTSEQ(*NONE) keyword specifies that the alternate collating sequence is not be used for comparisons involving the field. This keyword is valid for character data variables, such as data structures, subfields, stand-alone fields, parameters, etc.
ASCEND		The array or table data is in ascending sequence.
BASED	pointer variable	Identifies a pointer variable that holds the address (memory location) of variable being defined. The variable containing this keyword is be used to access the data pointed to.
CONST	literal value	Defines a Named Constant whose value is any valid character string or numeric literal or expression.
CONST		Indicates that the parameter being passed to the prototyped procedure or program is read-only. That is the called routine does not modify the parameter. In addition, CONST automatically converts values passed on the parameter to the type and size required by the parameter. For example, if a numeric parameter is defined as a 4-byte integer, CONST allows an expression, packed decimal, zoned numeric, or binary number to be specified. The value is automatically converted to the 4-byte integer data-type required by the parameter. The same is true of date variable. Specifying CONST allows the compiler to convert a date parameter from any valid date format, to the format required by the parameter.
CTDATA		Identifies the table or array as a compile time data table or array. The data for the table or array is stored near the bottom of the program and is identified by: **CTDATA *arrayname*

Keyword	Parameters	Description
DATFMT	format [*separator*]	Specifies the format to be used for the date field being defined. and literals used in the program. For example: DATFMT(*MDY/) If this keyword is not specified, the following hierarchy is used to determine the date format: The value specified for the DATFMT() keyword specified on the Header specification is used. If no DATFMT() keyword is specified on the Header specification, *ISO format (ccyy-mm-dd) is used. The separator character can be any character. If not specified, the default value (illustrated in Table 22 on page 59) is used.
DESCEND		The table or array data is in descending sequence.
DIM	number of elements	Identifies the number of elements in the table or array.
DTAARA	[data area name]	Associates the variable (data structure, data area data structure, or field) with the data area name. If the data area name is not specified, the name of the variable is issued as the data area name.
EXPORT		The variable (field or data structure) is available to other program modules linked (i.e., bound) into this program. Those other modules can use the IMPORT keyword to access the data for this variable. This provides an alternative to parameters when calling programs with the CALLB operation code.
EXTFLD	external fieldname	The external field name is renamed to the name specified in the *name* columns of the statement. The EXTFLD keyword is functionally equivalent to the DDS RENAME() keyword. To use this keyword, you must specify the letter E in column 22 of this Definition specification statement. If the PREFIX keyword is specified for the data structure, the prefix is not applied to this subfield.
EXTFMT	external format code	Identifies the external data type (format) of data loaded into pre-runtime arrays and tables.
EXTNAME	file name [: format]	For externally described data structures, the name of the file and optionally, the format name used to generate the data structure format. To use this keyword, you must specify the letter E in column 22 of this Definition specification statement.
EXTPGM	*program-name*	The name of the program whose prototype is being defined. The *program-name* can be a quoted character string or character field. If the *program-name* is not specified, the name specified in the name columns of the statement is used as the program name.

Keyword	Parameters	Description
EXTPROC	*procedure-name*	The name of the procedure whose prototype is being defined. The procedure-name can be a quoted character string, named constant or a procedure pointer. The procedure is an external procedure, meaning it is defined external to the program.
		If no procedure-name is specified, the name specified in the name columns of the statement is used as the procedure name.
		If the name specified for EXTPROC keyword begins with the letters "CEE" or an underscore ('_') character, the compiler treats it as a system built-in procedure. Meaning it generates the routine in-line, within the program. To avoid confusion with system provided APIs, never use the letter "Q" or the letters "CEE" as the prefix of a procedure name.
FROMFILE	file name	The name of the database file whose data will be used to load the pre-run time array or table.
IMPORT		The memory for the variable (field or data structure) is allocated in another program module. The data can be accessed from this program module. The definition of the variable should match that of the variable defined with the EXPORT keyword in the other program module.
INZ	initial value	The initial value for the variable. The value must be either a quoted character string, numeric literal, named constant, or an expression that can be analyzed at compile time.
LIKE	based-on variable	Used to assign the attribute of the based-on variable to the new variable. Only the size, decimal positions (if any) and data type are inherited. The initial value is not. See array dimensions for a tip on inheriting the dimensions of other arrays.
NOOPT		Prohibits optimization of the variable. Functionally similar to the VOLITILE keyword in the C language.
OCCURS	occurrences	The number of occurrences for the multiple occurrence data structure.
OPDESC		Causes the compiler to pass *operational descriptors* with the parameters that are defined within this prototype. This is the prototype-call interface version of the CALLB(D) operation extender.

Keyword	Parameters	Description
OPTIONS		Controls parameter options on a prototype.
	*OMIT	Indicates that a null value can be passed for the parameter. RPG IV uses *OMIT instead of *NULL as the null placeholder.
	*NOPASS	Indicates that the parameter is optional. All subsequent parameters must also have OPTIONS(*NOPASS) specified. This allows a prototype call to be evoked with a variable number of parameters.
	*VARSIZE	Indicates that the parameter accepts values shorter than the parameter definition. If OPTIONS(*VARSIZE) and the CONST keyword are not specified, the parameter must be at least as long as the parameter definition.
	*STRING	Indicates that a null-terminator (x'00') is added to the end of a character string expression passed to this parameter. OPTIONS(*STRING) requires that the parameter be of type pointer (*) and also include either the VALUE or CONST keyword.
OVERLAY	subfield [: start]	Causes the position of the subfield being defined to be located at start of the overlaid subfield.
PACKEVEN		Causes a Packed Decimal field to be packed with an even number of digits. That is, the decimal precision will be an even number of digits, such as, 2, 4, 6, 8 and so on. If this keyword is not specified, the field is packed with an even number of digits, such as : 3, 5, 7, 9, 11 and so on. Use this keyword with the From and To positions when defining a field and you want an even number of decimal positions.
PERRCD	entries per record	The number of elements per record for a compile-time or pre-runtime array. The default value for this keyword is 1.

Keyword	Parameters	Description
PREFIX	prefix [: *replace size*]	For Externally Described data structures, the PREFIX keyword is used to automatically rename all field names in the file specified by the EXTNAME() keyword. The prefix is appended to the beginning of each field name from the externally described file. The prefix cannot be enclosed in quotes. For example: PREFIX(CM) causes the fields: ACTNO, CUSTNM, and CUSTAD to be renamed to: CMACTNO, CMCUSTNM, and CMCUSTAD While PREFIX(CM_)causes those same fields to be renamed to: CM_ACTNO, CM_CUSTNM, and CM_CUSTAD. The optional *Replacement Size* can be used to trim off the first *n* characters from field names before appending the prefix. For example: PREFIX(CST_ : 2) causes the field named CMNAME to be renamed to: CST_NAME, and a field named ACTNO is renamed to: CST_TNO. Use this option with caution. Unlike the File specification PREFIX keyword, the Definition specification PREFIX keyword accepts prefixes up to 4095 bytes in length (one less than the RPG IV field name length limit).
PROCPTR		This keyword is used to indicate that a field of type pointer is being declared as a procedure pointer. A procedure pointer can be used in Factor 2 of the CALLB or CALLP operation codes.
STATIC		Indicates that the field, data structure, array or other stand-alone field defined within a subprocedure should be stored in so called *static storage*. This means that the field will retain its value after the subprocedure in which it is defined, ends. The keyword is only valid within a subprocedure. If STATIC is not specified, fields within subprocedures are destroyed (release back to the system) after the subprocedure ends. The next time the subprocedure is called, the non-STATIC fields are recreated, and initialized. Such fields are called automatic fields; that is they are stored in *automatic storage*. For subprocedures that are called recursively, each evocation of the subprocedure generates unique automatic variables, while maintaining the static variables throughout the program.
TIMFMT	format [: *separator*]	Specifies the format for time fields. If this keyword is not specified, the *ISO format (hh.mm.ss 24 hour clock) is used. The separator can be any character. If no separator is specified, the default value (illustrated in Table 23 on page 60) is used.

47

Keyword	Parameters	Description
TOFILE	file name	Identifies the output file for a pre-runtime array or table. The data from the array is written to this file when the program ends. The file must be defined on the File Description specifications as a Combined file, and must have a file designation of T (table).
VALUE		Indicates that the parameter is to be passed by value. Normally, in RPG, parameters are passed by reference. Only parameters passed to a procedure can be passed by value. When a parameter is passed by value, the called procedure receives its own copy of the parameter value. The called procedure normally does not change the parameter when it is passed by VALUE. The VALUE keyword cannot be specified for a parameter if its prototype was defined using the EXTPGM keyword.

Table 13: Definition Specification Keywords

Procedure Specification Keywords

Keyword	Parameters	Description
EXPORT		Indicates that the procedure being defined is available for importing by other modules. It is recommended that EXPORT be used on all procedures except those unique to the RPG source module being created. For example, a procedure that calculates a profit margin would be exported, but one that only marks up a price by 10 percent might not.

Table 13-A: Procedure Specification Keywords

Expressions

Expressions

There are two types of expressions, *numeric* and *string*. An expression is any list of tokens that represents a value, either a character string or numeric value. In other words, it's any character string or numeric statement.

RPG support for natural expressions is similar to that of CL, BASIC, COBOL, C++, and PL/I. Expressions can be used in extended Factor 2 of the Alternate Calculation specification, and in the keyword section of the Definition specification. Expressions can be used in assignment statements, compare statements, or in declarations.

Expressions are made up of literal values, numbers, fields, and symbols, known as *tokens*. Symbols are used to perform operations on the various values. An expression can be as simple as the number 12, or a complex as the equation: (4*PI)*R**2.

Table 14 contains a list of the symbols supported for expressions.

Symbol	Description
( )	Parentheses
**	Exponentiation (powers and roots are supported)
*	Multiplication
/	Division
+	Concatenation (in character string expressions only.)
+	Addition
-	Subtraction
NOT	Negates the result of the following expression

Table 14: Symbols Used in Expressions

Continuing An Expression

To continue an expression, simply place the next token of the expression on the next line in the Extended Factor 2, or the Function/Keyword area of the Definition specification.

To continue a character string expression, you can specify the next token, or break a quoted character string and continue it on the next line. When breaking a quoted character string, use either a + or - sign to continue the string. This directs the compiler to concatenate the value together either on the first non-blank position (using the plus + sign) or the first position of the Extended Factor 2 or Function/Keyword area (when using the minus - sign.)

Priority of Operators

Expressions are parsed, and then evaluated in a defined order. To ensure that the equation always results in the same value, a precedence of the operations is applied. Fortunately, this precedence is the same as that used by most other programming languages and as well as mathematics. Table 15 contains the priority of the operators used in expressions in RPG.

Symbols In Order of Priority	Description
( )	Parentheses
Built-in function	%SUBST(), %SIZE(), etc.
unary + and -	Plus and minus used as sign values
**	Powers and Roots
* and /	Multiplication and Division
+ and -	Addition and subtraction
Compare operators	=, >, <, >=, <=, <>
AND	Logical ANDing of two values
OR	Logical ORing of two values
NOT	Logical reversal of an expression
=	Assignment

Table 15: Expression Operator Priority

The priority of parentheses and built-in functions is interpreted as meaning that the operations inside the parentheses are performed independently of the operations outside the parentheses. Use parentheses for clarity. If you are not sure about the priority of the equation, parentheses can be used to override any existing priority. Hence, you can force the addition operation to be performed before a multiplication operation.

The Power function ** is used to raise a value to a power. Mathematical rules state that if a value is raised to the power of $1/n$ ("one over n",) the result is the nth root of the value. Table 16 illustrates a few sample equations that use powers and roots.

Equation	Description
4 ** 2	Results in 4 squared, or 4x4 (16).
4 ** .5	Results in the square root of 4 (2).
9 ** (1/3)	Finds the cubed root of 9 (3).
16 ** (1/2)	Finds the square root of 16 (4).

Table 16: Sample Use of Powers and Roots

Expressions in Assignment Statements

When one value is assigned to another, the EVAL operation code is used. This operation code copies the value on the right of the equal sign, known as the *r-value*, to the variable on the left of the equal sign, known as the *l-value*. The assignment must result in a matching *r-value* and *l-value*. That is, if the *l-value* is character, then the *r-value* must result in a character string.

The l-value can be an expression, but only when it is a character variable, or an array name with an index value. The %SUBST() built-in function can be used as the l-value. In addition, numeric expressions can be used on the starting position and the length of the %SUBST() function. When an array index is specified, the index may be a literal, a field, or an expression.

Table 17 contains a sample of several expressions used in assignment statements.

```
.....CSRn01Factor1+++++++OpCode(ex)Factor2+++++++++++++++++++++++++++++++++++++++
0001 C                    EVAL       A = B + C
0002 C                    EVAL       Amt_Due = Amt_Due - Amt_Paid
0003 C                    EVAL       PI = 3.1415926
0004 C                    EVAL       Area = 4 * PI * Radius ** 2
0005 C                    EVAL       Message = 'RPGIV is cool!'
0006 C                    EVAL       %subst(comp_name : str+3 : str+6) = 'Q38'
0007 C                    EVAL       ptrData = %ADDR(comp_name)
0008 C                    EVAL       Presidents(I + 1) = 'George ' + 'Washington'
```

Table 17: Sample Assignment Expressions

In Table 17, line 1 computes the sum of B plus C and stores the result in A. Line 2, the AMT_DUE field is reduced by AMT_PAID. Line 3, the field named PI receives the value of 3.1415926. Line 4, the area of a circle is computed as 4 x PI x R2

Line 5 copies a character string expression to the field named MESSAGE. Line 6 copies the character string expression 'Q38' to a substring location of the COMP_NAME field.

Line 7 retrieves the address of the field COMP_NAME, and copies it into the pointer variable named PTRDATA. Line 8 concatenates the string 'George ' 'Washington' into 'George Washington' and copies it into an array element of the PRESIDENTS array. The element index is calculated from the expression I+1.

Expressions in Compare Statements

The RPG operation code DOW, DOU, IF and WHEN allow the use of expressions in compare statements. Expressions used here do not assign their result to any value, but rather, it is used to compare one value to another.

The symbols in Table 18 below, describe the compare operands supported by RPG.

Compare Operands	Description
=	Equality
>	Greater than
<	Less than
>=	Greater than or Equal to
<=	Less than or Equal to
<>	Not Equal to
NOT	Reverse condition
AND	Continuation of condition
OR	Continuation of condition

Table 18: Compare Symbols

The DOW, DOU, WHEN, and IF operation codes have identical support for expressions. Table 19 illustrates various conditional expressions.

```
·.....CSRn01Factor1+++++++OpCode(ex)Factor2+++++++Result++++++++Len++DcHiLoEq....
.....CSRn01..............OpCode(ex)Extended-factor2++++++++++++++++++++++++++++++
0001 C                   if        A = B
0002 C                   if        Amt_Due > 10000 and DaysOvrDue >= 30
0003 C                   if        (Price - Cost) / Price < 10 or
0004 C                              Cost = 0
0005 C                   select
0006 C                   when      *IN01 = *ON
0007 C                   DOU       *INLR
0008 C                   read      Customer                              LR
0009 C                   endDo
0010 C                   endsel
```

Table 19: Conditional Expressions

Data Types

RPG Data Types

RPG supports a wide variety of data types, such as character, numeric, packed decimal, pointer and date and time. Data types are used to declare field and array element attributes. This attribute is specified in the data type column of the Definition specification, or inferred by the compiler when a variable is defined on the Calculation specification. Table 20 contains a description of the available data types supported by RPG.

Data Type Name	Data Type	Size Extent	Description
Character	A or blank	1 to 32,767	Character.
Date	D	8 or 10 bytes	Date. See also: *Time, Timestamp*
Floating Point	F	8-byte float	Floating point numeric.
Graphic (DBCS)	G	32,767	Double-byte character set / 'Graphic Data'.
Integer	I	2 or 4 bytes	Integer. See also: *Unsigned*
Left Signed	L	1 to 30	Signed numeric with sign on left side.
Named Indicator	N	1	Named Indicator.
Packed	P	1 to 30	Packed decimal.
Pointer	*	16 bytes	Pointer. See also: *PROCPTR* keyword
Right Signed	R	1 to 30	Signed numeric with sign on right side.
RPG Binary	B	2 or 4	RPG Binary 4 or 9 digits of accuracy.
Signed	S or blank	1 to 30	Signed numeric with integrated sign.
Time	T	8	Time. See also: *Date, TimeStamp*
TimeStamp	Z	26	Date/Time Stamp. See also: *Date, Time*
Unsigned Integer	U	2 or 4	Unsigned integer. See also: *Integer*

Table 20: Data Types

The Date and Time data types have special operation codes to support arithmetic operations. All others data types use the ADD and SUB operation codes. Date and Time data types, however, cannot be used with the ADD and SUB operation codes. Instead, the ADDDUR and SUBDUR operation codes are supported.

The ADDDUR operation is an easy way to add a duration to a date or time. For example, you can add 30 days to an invoice date, or add 8 hours to a start time.

The SUBDUR operation is more versatile than ADDDUR. In fact, SUBDUR can do everything ADDDUR can due. In addition, SUBDUR can be used to calculate the duration between 2 date values. The duration is stored in the Result field, and can be the number Days, Months, Years, or Hours, Minutes, or Seconds. See Date and Time Data Types beginning on page 57 for more information.

Date and Time Data Types

Three data types support dates. They are D (date), T (time) and Z (timestamp).

These data types are substantially different than signed numeric variables that contain date fields. Unlike earlier versions of RPG, RPGIV supports native *Date* and *Time* data types. You can copy the old types to the new date data type fields using the MOVE operation code.

```
.....DName++++++++++EUDSFrom+++To/Len+TDc.Functions++++++++++++++++++++++++++++
0001 D Inv_Date         S              D    DATFMT(*MDY/)
.....CSRn01Factor1+++++++OpCode(ex)Factor2+++++++Result++++++++Len++DcHiLoEq
0002 C* Convert from non-date to Date variable
0003 C     *MDY          MOVE      INVDAT          Inv_Date
```

Date data type variables are normally 8 or 10 positions in length. An 8 position date includes the month, day, and year, but not the century. A 10 position date includes the month, day, year, and the century. Time data types variables are always 8 positions in length.

The edit mask, or *separator* is included in the length of the variable. For example, the date February 17, 1995 is represented as '02-17-95' in a date variable with *MDY- specified as its format and separator. This is the external format of the date, that is the format that is visible to the RPG program. An internal format of a date value is not visible to the RPG program. This internal format is consistent regardless of the external format of a date or time variable. This allows the use of date and time variables in various formats to be used without concern to their external format. So a date with a format of *MDY can be subtracted from a date with a format of *ISO without worrying about the conversion.

Specifying Date / Time Literal Values

Date and time literals used in the program are preceded with the letter D for dates, and T for time. The date or time literal itself must be enclosed in single quotation marks, and must be in the format and contain the separator specified on the Header specification's DATFMT keyword.

Date / Time Format	Sample Literal Value
*ISO	D'1995-06-21'
*USA	D'06/21/1995'
*MDY	D'06/21/95'
*MDY-	D'06-21-95'
*HMS	T'15:30:00'
*USA	T'03:30 PM'

Table 21: Sample Date / Time Literals

Date and Time literal values can be specified on the Definition specification and the Calculation specification. Fields that are numeric or character and contain a value that is used in the same manor as a date or time value, are not specified the same way real DATE and TIME literal values are specified. Those non-date, non-time values are specified based on how you set up your database and program. It is easy to confuse a non-date field and corresponding literal value with a date variable and date literal. So, use caution when this situation arises.

NOTE: All date and time literal values <u>must</u> be specified in the format specified on the DATFMT keyword on the Header specification regardless of the format of the individual date or time field being initialized. If no DATFMT keyword is specified, then the RPG compiler inserts DATFMT(*ISO) which uses a CCYY-MM-DD (*century year-month-day*) format.

Date Formats

The format of a date variable represents how the data in the field is presented to a program or input field. It has no real bearing on how the date is stored internally in the database.

The RPG DATE data type is the letter 'D'. The AS/400 database (DB2 for OS/400) supports dates that are compatible with RPG. In the DDS source, a date database field is defined using the letter 'L' as its data type identifier.

Table 22 illustrates the supported date formats. If no separator character is specified, a default separator (the first separator listed in each of row of "Valid Separators") is used.

Date Format	Description	Format	Valid Separators[14]	Length	Sample
*CYMD	OS/400 CL standard	cyymmdd			
*MDY	Month, Day, Year	mm/dd/yy	/ - . , & 0	8	02/17/95
*DMY	Day, Month, Year	dd/mm/yy	/ - . , & 0	8	17/02/95
*YMD	Year, Month, Day	yy/mm/dd	/ - . , & 0	8	95/02/17
*JUL	Julian (year, day of year 1 - 365)	yy/ddd	/ - . , & 0	8	95/48
*ISO	International Standards Organization	ccyy-mm-dd	- 0	10	1995-02-17
*USA	IBM's USA Standard	mm/dd/ccyy	/ 0	10	02/17/1995
*EUR	IBM's European Standard	dd.mm.ccyy	. 0	10	17.02.1995
*JIS	Japanese Industrial Standard	ccyy-mm-dd	- 0	10	1995-02-17
*JOBRUN	OS/400 Job Format	same as job			
*JOB	OS/400 Job Format	N/A			
*SYS	OS/400 Job Format	N/A			

Table 22: Formats for Date Variables

*JOBRUN is used to convert between a numeric value (such as *DATE or UDATE) and a date variable.

*JOB and *SYS are used to initialize a date variable to the current job or system date respectively.

---

[14] The user of the 0 (zero) separator indicates that no separator is being used, or that none is requested.

Time Formats

The format for a TIME variable represents how the data in the TIME field is presented to a user or a program, or its format when it is being moved to/from another field. It has no real bearing on how the time is stored internally in the database.

Table 23 illustrates the supported formats for TIME variables. If no format is specified, the *ISO (International standards organization) format is used as the default format. If no separator character is specified, the default separator is used. The default separator is the colon in most formats (except *EUR). If the ampersand (&) is used, a blank is used as the separator.

Time Format	Description	Format	Valid Separators	Length	Sample
*HMS	Hours, Minutes, Seconds	hh:mm:ss	: . , &	8	15:30:00
*ISO	International Standards Organization	hh.mm.ss	.	8	15:30:00
*USA	IBM's USA Standard	hh:mm AM hh:mm PM	:	8	3:30 PM
*EUR	IBM's European Standard	hh.mm.ss	.	8	15:30:00
*JIS	Japanese Industrial Standard	hh:mm:ss	:	8	15:30:00

Table 23: Formats for TIME Variables

Date and Time Duration Codes

The date and time operation codes EXTRCT, ADDDUR, and SUBDUR allow you to specify a duration code or extraction value. For example, you can subtract one date from another and have the Result field value be the number of days between the two dates, the number of months between the two dates, and so on. Table 24 below identifies the duration codes.

Duration Code	Short Hand	Description
*YEARS	*Y	Years
*MONTHS	*M	Months
*DAYS	*D	Days
*HOURS	*H	Hours
*MINUTES	*MN	Minutes
*SECONDS	*S	Seconds
*MSECONDS	*MS	Microseconds

Table 24: Duration Codes

Use one of these duration codes in Factor 2 along with the corresponding value for the ADDDUR, SUBDUR and EXTRCT operations.

Date and Time Operation Codes

There are five operation codes that support manipulation of date and time values. These include operation codes to perform date/time arithmetic, extraction, and validation.

ADDDUR (Add Duration)

Use this operation code to add a time or period to a date or time variable. For example, use ADDDUR to add 30 days to an invoice date.

SUBDUR (Subtract Duration)

Use this operation code to find the time or period between two dates or two times. For example, subtract a due date from today's date to calculate the number of days past due for an invoice.

EXTRCT (Extract Date/Time Component)

Use this operation code to retrieve the components of date, time or timestamp variable. You can extract the hours, minutes, seconds, or microseconds, or the year, month, or day.

MOVE (Move Date/Convert Date)

Use this operation code to convert between date or time values and character or numeric fields.

TIME (Get Current Date/Time)

Use this operation code to retrieve the current system date, time or timestamp. The Result field can be a numeric, character, date, time or timestamp variable.

TEST (Test for Valid Date/Time)

Use this operation code to validate any type of field for a valid date, time or timestamp value.

Pointers and Dynamic Memory

The use of pointer variables in RPG is a new concept. RPG programs typically use automatic storage and full compile-time field definitions. RPG provides support for pointers, addressing and dynamic memory.

Pointers are fields with a data type of *pointer*. The asterisk (*) is used in RPG to indicate the pointer data type. The Definition specifications are used to declare a pointer field. A pointer can be declared just like any other field, therefore it can be a stand-alone field, an array element, data structure subfield, or parameter.

A pointer field can contain a memory address. In RPG, this would typically be the address of another field in the program, or the address of a subprocedure. In addition, the memory address returned by the ALLOC operation is stored in a pointer field.

To move the address of another field into a pointer field, the %ADDR built-in function is provided. Specify the name of the field whose address you want to store, within the parentheses of the %ADDR built-in function. Use %ADDR on the Definition specification with the INZ keyword, or as a component of a expression with any operation code that supports expressions.

The BASED keyword is used to indicate the name of a field that is used to access the data stored at a pointer location. That is, if field A is based on pointer P, then the data located at the address stored in P, is available to the RPG program by referring to A.

Pointers can also be used to store the address of so called *dynamic memory*. Dynamic memory is memory outside the normal scope of the program. That is, it is not declared as a field or data structure within the program itself, but is allocated at runtime by the program.

Three operation codes provide support for dynamic memory management. ALLOC (allocate) is used to dynamically allocate a specific number of bytes. The address of the allocated memory is stored in a pointer field. REALLOC (reallocate) is used when the number of bytes allocated by an ALLOC operation needs to be changed (increased or decreased). REALLOC allocates the new memory size, and copies the original data to the new location. DEALLOC (release allocated memory) releases memory previously allocated by the ALLOC or REALLOC operations.

ALLOC   (Allocate Memory)

The ALLOC operation code allocates memory from the system for the number of bytes specified in Factor 2. The address of this newly allocated memory is stored in the pointer variable specified in the Result field.

Factor 1	OpCode	Factor 2	Result	Length	Dec	Resulting Indicators
	ALLOC	length	pointer			[error]

Factor 2 is required and must contain the number of bytes to be allocated. This can be a numeric literal or a numeric field whose value ranges from 1 to 16776704.

The result field must contain a pointer field. The address of the allocated memory is stored in the Result field.

Resulting indicator 2 is optional, and can be used to signal allocation failure. When the ALLOC operation fails, the Result field is not changed.

```
.....F*ileName++IFEASFRlen+LKeylnKFDevice+.Functions+++++++++++++++++++++++++++
0001 FCUSTMAST  IF   E              DISK     Infds(Cust_DS)

.....D*ame+++++++++++EUDS.......Length+TDc.Functions+++++++++++++++++++++++++++
0002 D Cust_DS           DS
0003 D RecdCount               156    159B 0

0004 D MAXREC            C                    CONST(32766)
0005 D Customer          S              7P 0 Dim(MAXREC) based(pCust)

0006 D nBytes            S              9P 0
0007 D pCust             S               *

.....C*Rn01..............OpCode(ex)Extended-factor2+++++++++++++++++++++++++++++
0008 C                   IF       RecdCount < MAXREC
0009 C                   Eval     nBytes = RecdCount * %size(Customer)  + 1

0010 C                   ALLOC    nBytes        pCust                      73

0011 C                   Do       RecdCount     X                     7 0
0012 C                   Read     CustRec                                 LR
0013 C                   IF       NOT *INLR
0014 C                   Eval     Customer(x) = CustNum
0015 C                   endif
0016 C                   enddo
0017 C                   endif
0018 C                   move     *ON           *inLR
```

Table 25: Example Dynamic Memory Allocation

In this example, the number of records in the CUSTMAST file is used to calculate the number of bytes of memory needed. Since the CUSTOMER array (line 5) contains 7-digit packed decimal elements, each element uses 4-bytes of memory. To calculate the number bytes needed to dynamically allocate elements for this array, the number of desired elements needs to be multiplied by 4 (line 10).

REALLOC   (Re-Allocate Memory)

The REALLOC operation code allocates memory from the system for the number of bytes specified in Factor 2. The address of this newly allocated memory is stored in the pointer field specified in the Result field. Unlike the ALLOC operation, however, the pointer field specified in the Result field must already contain the address of a previously allocated memory location. The contents of the original location are copied to the new location, and the original memory is released (deallocated).

Factor 1	OpCode	Factor 2	Result	Length	Dec	Resulting Indicators
	REALLOC	length	pointer			[error]

Factor 2 is required and must contain the number of bytes to be allocated. This can be a numeric literal or a numeric field whose value ranges from 1 to 16776704.

The Result field must contain a pointer field. The address of the allocated memory is stored in the Result field. The Result field must already contain a valid memory address from a previous run ALLOC or REALLOC operation.

Resulting indicator 2 is optional, and can be used to signal reallocation failure. When the reallocate fails, the Result field is not changed.

Memory is allocated to equal the number of bytes specified for the length in Factor 2. The data from the original location is copied to the new memory location. The original memory location is then released back to the system.

```
.....Dname+++++++++++EUDS.......Length+TDc.Functions++++++++++++++++++++++++++++
0001 D szData            S            2000A    based(pData)
0002 D pData             S               *

.....CsrN01Factor1+++++++OpCode(ex)Factor2+++++++Result++++++++Len++DcHiLoEq....
0003 C                   Alloc      1000         pData
0004 C                   Eval       %subst(szData : 1 : 1000) = 'Some value'

0005 C                   REALLOC    2000         pData
```

Table 26: Example Dynamic Memory ReAllocation

DEALLOC   (Deallocate Memory)

The DEALLOC operation code allocates memory from the system for the number of bytes specified in Factor 2. The address of this newly allocated memory is stored in the pointer field specified in the Result field. Unlike the ALLOC operation, however, the pointer field specified in the Result field must already contain the address of a previously allocated memory location. The contents of the original location are copied to the new location, and the original memory is released (deallocated).

Factor 1	OpCode	Factor 2	Result	Length	Dec	Resulting Indicators
	DEALLOC(N)		pointer			[error]

Factor 2 is required and must contain the number of bytes to be allocated. This can be a numeric literal or a numeric field whose value ranges from 1 to 16776704.

The Result field must contain a pointer that contains a value previously set by an ALLOC or REALLOC operation. The pointer must be set to the beginning of the allocated memory.

The operational extender N, if specified, sets the pointer in the Result field to *NULL after a successful deallocation.

Resulting indicator 2 is optional, and can be used to signal deallocation failure. When the DEALLOC operation fails, the pointer value in the Result field is not changed. If the pointer field contains *NULL, the operation is ignored.

Note: On the IBM AS/400, the Integrated Language Environment (ILE) insures that allocated memory is contained to within an Activation Group boundary. As with any system, however, there are ways to circumvent this safety feature.

Editing Numeric Data

Edit Words

Edit words are patterns or *masks* that are specified in RPG Output specifications. They are used to create ad hoc edits for numeric values such as phone numbers, social security numbers, sales figures and the time-of-day. Table 27 illustrates various edit word masks.

Description	Edit Word *...v....1....v..	Unedited Value	Edited Output
Large value	`'    ,    .'`	00654321	6,543.21
Stop zero-suppression	`'    , 0 .'`	00000027	0.27
Time-of-day	`'0 :  :  '`	071223	07:12:23
Social Security number	`'0  -  -    '`	023456789	023-45-6789
Phone number	`'0( )&  -    '`	8005529404	(800) 552-9404
Floating currency symbol	`'    ,   , $0.'`	000009402	$94.02

Table 27: Sample Edit Word Usage

The number of blanks plus the zero suppression control code (i.e., the leading zero or asterisk), within an edit word must be greater than or equal to the number of digits for the field or named constant being edited.

TIP: To prevent zero suppression of output, specify a leading zero in the first (i.e., leftmost) position of the edit word. This is typically used for editing values such as phone numbers where zero suppression is not desired. This technique, however, applies only to RPG and not to AS/400 DDS.

The currency symbol and zero suppression character do not displace numbers within the edit word. The currency symbol, however, requires an additional position. This additional position is usually allocated as the leftmost position of the edit word. Table 28 illustrates the edit mask required to edit a numeric field with a floating currency symbol, commas, a decimal point and zero suppression. The size of this numeric field is 9 positions with 2 decimal positions.

Output positions ·	CS	1		2	3	4		5	6	7		8	9	
Edit Word mask ·	'	ƀ	ƀ	,	ƀ	ƀ	ƀ	,	ƀ	$	0	.	ƀ	ƀ	'
Unedited value ·					7	6	5		4	3	2	1	2	1	
Output value ·	$	7		,	6	5	4	,	3	2	1	.	2	1	

Table 28: Edit Mask with Floating Currency Symbol

Edit words consist of four optional elements:

1. The *Body*. The area of the edit word where the numeric value will be positioned.

2. The *Status*. The area of the edit word consisting of the letters CR or a minus sign (-). It is used to indicate whether the value is negative or positive.

3. The *Expansion*. The area following the body and status (usually literal values).

4. *Literal values*. Literal values can appear anywhere in the edit word. Literal values are included in the output only when significant digits appear to the left of the literal value. Note: While a named constant can be used as a complete edit word, named constants cannot be used within the edit word itself.

Edit Word Control Codes

There are several control codes that can be inserted into an edit word to control zero suppression, leading asterisks, floating currency symbol, blanks and decimal notation. The first occurrence of a *control code* is used as the control code. Subsequent occurrences are treated as literal values except for the ampersand (&), which is always used as a control code. Table 29 contains a description of the edit word control codes that can be used in an edit word.

Control Code	Description
$	**Currency symbol**: If the currency symbol is followed immediately by a zero, the currency symbol will precede the first significant digit. This is referred to as a floating currency sign. If the currency symbol is not followed by a zero, the currency symbol's position is fixed. When using the floating currency symbol, an available blank position is displaced. Typically, the displaced blank is shifted to the left of the currency symbol. The character used as the currency symbol is specified in column 18 of the Header specification.
*	**Asterisk**: Leading zeros are replaced with asterisks through the position of the asterisk. Zero suppression ends at the position of the asterisk.
&	**Ampersand**: Always replaced with a blank when output.
0	**Zero**: Ends zero suppression at the position of the zero. The zero is used as one of the output positions where digits to appear.
. or ,	**Decimal notation**: These characters are not actual control codes. They are treated as literal values and are traditionally used as decimal or thousands notation.
ƀ	**Blanks**: Identifies available positions for the numeric value.
CR	**Status**: The literal value CR is output if the value is negative.
-	**Status**: The minus sign (-) is output if the value is negative.

Table 29: Edit Word Control Codes

Edit Words and Named Constants

To use an edit word, place the desired edit word—left-justified—into columns 53 through 80 of the Output specification for the field being edited. The RPG Output specification accepts edit word literal values of up to 28 positions. For edit words that exceed 28 positions, a Named Constant can be used. Named constant edit words can be up to 115 positions in length and can be specified–left justified–in columns 53 to 80 of the Output specification. Table 30 contains several samples of edit word usage.

```
.....FFilename++IPEASFRlen+LKlen+AIDevice+.Functions++++++++++++++++++++++++++++
      FQPRINT    O   F  132        PRINTER OFLIND(OV)
.....DName++++++++++EUDSFrom+++To/Len+TDc.Functions++++++++++++++++++++++++++++++
      D EditPhone         C                 Const('0(   )&    -     ')
.....CSRn01Factor1+++++++OpCode(ex)Factor2+++++++Result++++++++Len++DcHiLoEq....
      C                  TIME                     TIME           6 0
      C                  Z-ADD    *DATE           DATE           9 0
      C                  Z-ADD    8005551212      PHONE         10 0
      C                  Z-ADD    654321          SALES         10 2
      C                  MOVE     023456789       SSNBR          9 0
      C                  EXCEPT
      C                  SETON                                      LR
.....OFormat++++DAddn01n02n03Except++++SpbSpaSkbSka............................
      OQPRINT    E                              1
.....O.............n01n02n03Field+++++++++YB?End++PConstant/Editword++++++++++
      O                                       +  0 'Soc Sec Nbr:'
      O                  SSNBR                +  2 '0   -   -     '
      O                                       +  2 'Phone Nbr:'
      O                  PHONE                +  2 EditPhone
      O                                       +  2 'Date/Time:'
      O                  DATE          Y      +  2
      O                  TIME                 +  2 '0  &  &  '
      O                                       +  2 'Salary:'
      O                  SALES                +  2 '$  ,    ,    *. CR'
```

Table 30: Sample Edit Word Usage

TIP: Use caution when using literal values in an edit word. Literal values can be any characters, including the letters CR. The first occurrence of the letters CR is interpreted as the *status* code and do not appear when the output value is positive.

Edit Codes

Edit codes are single-character codes that represent predefined editing patterns. These edit patterns are edit word masks that automatically adapt to the size of the numeric field or named constant being edited. This allows numeric fields of any size to be edited without concern for the particular semantics involved in using edit words.

To edit using an edit code, place the desired edit code into column 44 of the Output specification for the field to be edited.

Edit codes can be combined with special edit characters, such as the floating currency symbol ($) and leading asterisk (*), to further edit numeric output. These special characters can be specified—left justified—in columns 53 through 80 of the Output specification. The characters must be enclosed in single quotes (i.e., apostrophes), and only one of these characters can be specified for a field edited with an edit code.

To illustrate the output of numeric values edited with edit codes, three versions of edited output are illustrated in Table 31. The first uses only the edit code, the second uses the edit code and the floating currency symbol, and the third uses the edit code with leading asterisks.

In each sample, the data being output is a nine-digit numeric field with two decimal positions. For sample output of positive numbers, the value 0004567.89 is used; for negative output, the value -0004567.89 is used; and for zero output, the value 0000000.00 is used.

Edit Code	Thousands Notation	Output Zeros If Zero	Negative Sign	Sample Positive Output	Sample Negative Output	Sample Zero Output
1	Yes	Yes	No	4,567.89	4,567.89	.00
1 '$'				$4,567.89	$4,567.89	$.00
1 '*'				****4,567.89	****4,567.89	*********.00
2	Yes	No	No	4,567.89	4,567.89	
2 '$'				$4,567.89	$4,567.89	
2 '*'				****4,567.89	****4,567.89	************
3	No	Yes	No	4567.89	4567.89	.00
3 '$'				$4567.89	$4567.89	$.00
3 '*'				****4567.89	****4567.89	*********.00
4	No	No	No	4567.89	4567.89	
4 '$'				$4567.89	$4567.89	
4 '*'				****4567.89	****4567.89	**********
A	Yes	Yes	Yes CR	4,567.89	4,567.89CR	.00
A '$'				$4,567.89	$4,567.89CR	$.00
A '*'				****4,567.89	****4,567.89CR	*********.00
B	Yes	No	Yes CR	4,567.89	4,567.89CR	

Edit Code	Thousands Notation	Output Zeros If Zero	Negative Sign	Sample Positive Output	Sample Negative Output	Sample Zero Output
B '$'				$4,567.89	$4,567.89CR	
B '*'				****4,567.89	****4,567.89CR	************
C	No	Yes	Yes CR	4567.89	4567.89CR	.00
C '$'				$4567.89	$4567.89CR	$.00
C '*'				****4567.89	****4567.89CR	*******.00
D	No	No	Yes CR	4567.89	4567.89CR	
D '$'				$4567.89	$4567.89CR	
D '*'				****4567.89	****4567.89CR	************
J	Yes	Yes	Yes –	4,567.89	4,567.89-	.00
J '$'				$4,567.89	$4,567.89-	$.00
J '*'				****4,567.89	****4,567.89-	*********.00
K	Yes	No	Yes –	4,567.89	4,567.89-	
K '$'				$4,567.89	$4,567.89-	
K '*'				****4,567.89	****4,567.89-	************
L	No	Yes	Yes –	4567.89	4567.89-	.00
L '$'				$4567.89	$4567.89-	$.00
L '*'				****4567.89	****4567.89-	*******.00
M	No	No	Yes –	4567.89	4567.89-	
M '$'				$4567.89	$4567.89-	
M '*'				****4567.89	****4567.89-	************
N	Yes	Yes	Yes –	4,567.89	-4,567.89	.00
N '$'				$4,567.89	-$4,567.89	$.00
N '*'				****4,567.89	****-4,567.89	*********.00
O	Yes	No	Yes –	4,567.89	-4,567.89	
O '$'				$4,567.89	-$4,567.89	
O '*'				****4,567.89	****-4,567.89	************
P	No	Yes	Yes –	4567.89	-4567.89	.00
P '$'				$4567.89	-$4567.89	$.00
P '*'				****4567.89	****-4567.89	*******.00
Q	No	No	Yes –	4567.89	-4567.89	
Q '$'				$4567.89	-$4567.89	
Q '*'				****4567.89	****-4567.89	************
X	No	Yes	No	000456789	00045678R	000000000
Y	No	Yes	N/A	45/67/89	N/A	0/00/00
Z	No	No	No	456789	456789	

Table 31: Sample Edit Code Usage

Edit Code Control Characteristics

The RPG Header specification is used to control global editing values. The currency symbol, date format, date separator, and decimal notation are all controlled by the Header specification. Table 32 describes the set of Header Specification keywords that control editing in RPG.

Keyword	Value	Description
CURSYM	Blank	Default currency symbol ($) is used.
	Any character	The specified character is used as the currency symbol. This entry must be quoted and cannot contain the following characters: zero (0); asterisk (*); comma (,); period (.); ampersand (&); minus sign (-); the letters C and R.
DATFMT	Not specified	The date format is *ISO.
	*MDY	month-day-year (mmddyy)
	*DMY	day-month-year (ddmmyy)
	*YMD	year-month-day (yymmdd)
	*JUL	Julian (yyddd)
	*ISO	International Standard Organization. century-year-month-day (ccyy-mm-dd)
	*USA	USA Standard. month-day-century-year (mm/dd/ccyy)
	*EUR	European Standard. day-month-century-year (ddmmccyy)
	*JIS	Japanese Industrial Standard. century-year-month-day (ccyymmdd)
DATEDIT	fmt[sep] *DMY *MDY *YMD	The format for numeric fields edited with the Y edit code. Only these three formats are supported. The separator character can be any character, and defaults to the forward slash. If a blank is desired, use the ampersand (&).
DECEDIT	Unspecified	Numeric fields use the period for decimal notation and the comma for thousands notation.
	'.'	Decimal notation is a period, leading zeros are suppressed.
	','	Decimal notation is a comma, leading zeros are suppressed.
	'0.'	Decimal notation is a period, leading zeros are printed.
	'0,'	Decimal notation is a comma, leading zeros are printed.

Table 32: Header Specification Edit-Related Keyword

Custom Currency Symbol

The character specified by the CURSYM() keyword on the Header specification is used as the currency symbol and can be used with edit words and edit codes. For example, if the "at" sign ('@') is specified, the @ symbol must be used as the currency symbol throughout the program. Table 33 illustrates the use of the @ symbol as the currency symbol.

```
.....HFunctions++++++++++++++++++++++++++++++++++++++++++++++++++++++++++++++++
0001 H CURSYM('@')
0002 H DATFMT(*MDY/)
.....fFilename++IPEASFRlen+LKlen+AIDevice+.Functions++++++++++++++++++++++++++++
0003 FQPRINT    O  F  132         PRINTER OFLIND(OV)
0004
.....OFormat++++DAddn01n02n03Except++++SpbSpaSkbSka
0005 OQPRINT     E                          1
.....O..............n01n02n03Field+++++++++YB?End++PConstant/Editword+++++++++++
0006 O                                  +   0 'Salary:'
0007 O                        Wages     B + 2 '   ,   , @0.   '
```

Table 33: Sample Custom Currency Symbol Usage

The currency symbol @ is identified on line 1 with the CURSYM() keyword. It is then used in Output specifications on line 7.

Also, note on line 2 that the DATFMT() keyword is used to establish the default date format for date literals, and date variables used in the program. If the DATFMT() keyword is not used, then DATFMT(*ISO) is used as the default.

Compiler Directives

Directive Syntax

The RPG compiler directives and SQL preprocessor directives provide functions to alter the RPG program listing and to include the SAA SQL database manager. The RPG directives are listed in Table 34.

With the exception of the /COPY compiler directive, most RPG compiler directives offer little additional function. The /COPY compiler directive allows external source members to be included at compile-time.

Directive	Description
`/COPY [[library/]file,]member`	Causes the compiler to include source code contained in a separate source member. Any RPG source code can be included using the /COPY directive, except another /COPY directive.
`/EJECT`	Causes the compiler to skip to the top of the next page when the compiled program is printed.
`/TITLE text`	Causes the compiler to print the text on the top of each page of the printed compiler list. Subsequent /TITLE directives override previous /TITLE.
`/SPACE [n]`	Causes the compiler to print n blank lines. If n is not specified, 1 is assumed. Range(1 to 112)
`/EXEC SQL [sql statement]`	This SQL preprocessor directive starts an SQL statement. The SQL statement can begin on this line or on a subsequent line.
`+ continued-sql statement`	This SQL preprocessor directive indicates the continuation of the SQL statement that began with /EXEC SQL.
`/END-EXEC`	This SQL preprocessor directive ends the SQL statement that followed the previous /EXEC SQL.
`/DEFINE`	This directive defines a precompiler symbol.
`/UNDEFINE`	This directive undefines a precompiler symbol.l
`/IF`	Indicates that a condition is tested and if true, the block of statements below the /IF directive are processed (included) by the compiler.
`/ELSEIF`	Indicates that if the condition of the previous /IF directive is false, control transfers to this /ELSEIF directive and its condition is tested.
`/ELSE`	Indicates that if the condition of the /IF directive is false, control transfers to this /ELSE directive.
`/ENDIF`	Indicates the end of a code block enclosed by a previous /IF directive.
`/EOF`	Inserts an artificial end-of-file control. The compiler does not process any source statements beyond the /EOF directive.

Table 34: Preprocessor/Compiler Directives

Directive Samples

The sample program below illustrates the use of several RPG compiler directives. Since RPG does not generate errors when a line is blank (as RPGIII, RPGII and RPG do,) the use of /SPACE is limited.

```
0001  /TITLE Sample RPG Source with Directives
.....FFilename++IPEASFRlen+LKlen+AIDevice+.Functions++++++++++++++++++++++++++++
0002 FDSPFILE   CF  E                WORKSTN INFDS(wsds)
0003 FQPRINT    O   F  132           PRINTER PRTCTL(PRTCTL:*compat)
0004  /SPACE
.....DDame++++++++++ETDsFrom+++To/L+++IDc.Functions++++++++++++++++++++++++++++++
0005 D Hstruct         DS
0006 D  CustNumber                  5S 0
0007 D  CustName                   30A
0008 D  PhoneNo                    10S 0
0009
0010 D EditPhone       C                    Const('0(   )&   -   ')
0011 D KeyValue        S            5P 0
0012
0013  /COPY QINCSRC,STDDCL
0014
.....CSRn01Factor1+++++++OpCode(ex)Factor2+++++++Result++++++++Len++DcHiLoEq....
0015
0016 C                 Eval      KeyValue = 1207
0017 C/SQL EXEC
0018 C+         SELECT custnbr, custnam, phone FROM CUSTMAST
0019 C+          WHERE custnbr = :KEYValue
0020 C+          INTO :HStruct
0021 C/END EXEC
0022 C                 TIME                  TIME          6 0
0023 C                 Z-ADD     *DATE       DATE          9 0
0024 C                 EXCPT
0025 C                 MOVE      *ON         *INLR
0026 C/EJECT
```

Continued on next page.

Continued from previous page.

```
.....OFormat++++DAddn01n02n03Except++++SpbSpaSkbSka
0027 OQPRINT    E                      1
.....O..............n01n02n03Field+++++++++YB?End++PConstant/Editword++++++++++
0028 O                                      +  0 'Customer:'
0029 O                      CustNumber    Z  +  2
0030 OQPRINT    E                      1
0031 O                                      +  0 'Name:'
0032 O                      CustName       +  2
0033 OQPRINT    E                      1
0034 O                                      +  0 'Phone:'
0035 O                      PHONE          +  2 EditPhone
0036 OQPRINT    E                      1
0037 O                                      +  0 'Date/Time:'
0038 O                      DATE         Y  +  2
0039 O                      TIME           +  2 '0  :  :  '
```

Table 35: Sample Program to Illustrate RPG Compiler Directives

TIP1:   Use the /EJECT directive just before the first subroutine in the program; this provides a simple way to isolate subroutines from the rest of the program.

TIP2:   Use /COPY to include standard routines, data structures, and named constants. For example, a source member named STDDCL can be used to store frequently used constants, while another can be used to store the program status data structure, INFDS, or WSDS.

The Modern RPG IV Language Reference Summary

Program Status
and File Information
Data Structures

The Program Status Data Structure (PSDS) contains program-wide information, such as the number of parameters passed to the program when it is called, an error message ID, the name of the program at runtime, as well as other job information. There can be one PSDS per RPG program.

The File Information Data Structure (INFDS) contains vast amounts of file-specific information, from number of records in the file when the file is opened, to the file exceptions that occur.

To assign a data structure as the INFDS for a file, use the INFDS() keyword and specify the name of a data structure as its parameter.

For more information on how to specify File Continuation keywords see *File Continuation Keywords* beginning on page 38.

The PSDS is a normal data structure, but its name is special, or rather, the name "PSDS" is recognized by RPG and treated specially.

The PSDS is updated when the program is run and when an exception/error condition is detected. The INFDS is updated after each block of records is read from the file, or when a POST operation is performed on the file associated with the INFDS.

If a file is processed sequentially, often the INFDS will contain "old" information. For example, the INFDS may contain an incorrect relative record number for a file as the INFDS is updated only during the last blocked I/O, not necessarily the last record I/O.

Program Status Data Structure

Positions From To		Format Size	Description
*STATUS		Dec(5,0)	Status code.
*ROUTINE		Char(8)	RPG cycle routine that was active when the current exception/error occurred.
*PARMS		Dec(3,0)	Number of parameters passed to this program.
*PROC		Char(10)	Name of this procedure (i.e., program name.)
1	10	Char(10)	Name of this procedure (same as subfield *PROC).
11	15	Dec(5,0)	Status code (same as subfield *STATUS).
16	20	Dec(5,0)	Previous status code.
21	28	Char(8)	RPG source program statement number being processed when the exception/error occurred.
29	36	Char(8)	RPG cycle routine that was active when the current exception/error occurred (same as subfield *ROUTINE).
37	39	Dec(3,0)	Number of parameters passed to this program (same as subfield *PARMS).
40	42	Char(3)	Exception/error message ID prefix. Typically, CPF is used for OS/400 messages, and MCH is used for low-level system errors.
43	46	HEX(4)	This 4-position subfield contains the exception/error message ID suffix. A suffix number can be 0000 through FFFF, hexadecimal.
47	50	Char(4)	MI/ODT number. The number is the MI instruction number that relates to the RPG source program statement number in positions 21 through 28 of this data structure.
51	80	Char(30)	Reserved for exception/error message use.
81	90	Char(10)	Name of the library containing this program—at runtime.
91	170	Char(80)	The first-level text of the exception/error message that was issued.
171	174	Char(4)	Exception/error number for the exception/error that caused a called RPG program to fail.
175	200	Char(26)	Reserved.
201	208	Char(8)	File name accessed prior to an exception/error being issued.
209	243	Char(35)	Status information from the INFDS for the last file used prior to an exception/error being issued.
244	253	Char(10)	Job name of the job being run.
254	263	Char(10)	User Profile ID of the user profile that started the RPG program.
264	269	Dec(6,0)	Job number of the job being run.
270	275	Dec(6,0)	Start date—that is the date the program started running. The format of this subfield is the same as UDATE.
276	281	Dec(6,0)	System date—that is the date known to the computer. The format of this subfield is the same as UDATE.

Positions From	To	Format Size	Description
282	287	Dec(6,0)	Start time—that is the time the program started running. The format of this subfield is hhmmss.
288	293	Char(6)	Program creation date—that is the date the program was compiled. The format of this subfield is the same as UDATE. Its data type is character because that's how it is stored in the program.
294	299	Char(6)	Program creation time—that is the time the program was compiled. The format this subfield is hhmmss. Its data type is character
300	303	Char(4)	Compiler level.
304	313	Char(10)	Source file used to create this program.
314	323	Char(10)	Source file library used to create this program.
324	333	Char(10)	Source file member name used to create this program.
		Char(10)	Name of the program that activated this procedure.
		Char(255)	Name of the module containing this procedure.
		Date(8)	Date/Time stamp.

Table 36: Program Status Data Structure (PSDS)

File Information Data Structure

Positions From To		Type (size)	Description
*FILE		Char(8)	File name from the File Description specification to which this INFDS is assigned.
*INP		Dec(2,0)	National language input capability of the device file.
*MODE		Dec(2,0)	Preferred national language mode of the device file.
*OUT		Dec(2,0)	National language output capability of the device file.
*OPCODE		Char(6)	RPG operation code last used to access the file. If Factor 2 of the operation code contained a file name, the letter 'F' is appended to the operation stored in these positions; if Factor 2 of the operation code contains a record format name, the letter 'R' is appended to the operation stored in these positions; if the operation was an implicit file operation, (e.g., the RPG cycle read the file) the letter 'I' is appended to the operation stored in these positions.
*SIZE		Dec(4,0)	For WORKSTN device files, these positions contain the number of available positions on the display device when the WORKSTN device file is opened.
*STATUS		Dec(5,0)	Status code for the file to which this INFDS is assigned.
*RECORD		Char(8)	For program described files, the record identifying indicator of the record just processed is stored (left justified) in this subfield. For externally described files, the name of the record format just processed is stored in this subfield.
*ROUTINE		Char(8)	The name of the RPG cycle routine that was being performed when an exception/error occurred. The values that can be returned are as follows: *INIT Program initialization; *DETC Detail-time calculations; *DETL Detail-time output; *GETIN Get input record; *TOTC Total-time calculations; *TOTL Total-time output; *OFL Overflow output; *TERM Program end; program-name (called program named: first 8-characters only)
1	8	Char(8)	File name from the File Description specification to which this INFDS is assigned (same as subfield *FILE).
9	9	Char(1)	Open indication: '1' = Open; any other value = closed.
10	10	Char(1)	End of File indication: '1' = End of File; any other value = not EOF.
11	15	Dec(5,0)	Status code (same as subfield *STATUS).
16	21	Char(6)	Operation code (same as subfield *OPCODE).

Positions From	To	Type (size)	Description
22	29	Char(8)	Name of RPG routine in which exception/error occurred (same as subfield *ROUTINE).
30	37	Char(8)	This program's source statement number.
38	45	Char(8)	For program described files, the record identifying indicator of the record just processed is stored (left justified) in this subfield. For externally described files, the name of the record format just processed is stored in this subfield (same as subfield *RECORD).
46	52	Char(7)	Message identification number. (OS/400 message ID.)
53	56	Char(4)	MI/ODT number. The number is the MI instruction number to relates to the RPG source program statement number in positions 30 through 37 of this data structure.
57	66	Char(10)	Reserved.
67	70	Dec(4,0)	Number of positions for a WORKSTN device (same as subfield *SIZE).
71	72	Dec(2,0)	National language input capability of the device file (same as subfield *INP).
73	74	Dec(2,0)	Preferred national language mode of the device file (same as subfield *OUT).
75	76	Dec(2,0)	National language output capability of the device file (same as subfield *MODE).
81	82	Char(2)	Type of open data path (ODP). Valid choices are as follows: DS File is a Device File DB File is a Database file member SP File is a Spooled output file
83	92	Char(10)	Actual name of the file being processed (opened).
93	102	Char(10)	Actual name of the library contain the file being processed.
103	112	Char(10)	Spooled file name. Valid when positions 81 and 82 of this data structure contain 'SP'.
113	122	Char(10)	Spooled file library name. Valid when positions 81 and 82 of this data structure contain 'SP'.
123	124	Bin(2)	Spooled file number. Valid when positions 81 and 82 of this data structure contain 'SP'.
125	126	Bin(2)	Record length of the file being processed.
127	128	Bin(2)	Reserved.
129	138	Char(10)	Member name of the file being processed. Valid when positions 81 and 82 of this data structure contain either 'SP' or 'DB'. When MBR(*ALL) is specified for an OVRDBF command, this value is updated as the first record of each member is read.

Positions From	To	Type (size)	Description
139	142	Bin(4)	Reserved.
143	146	Bin(4)	Reserved.
147	148	Bin(2)	File type: 1 = Workstation (display) device file 2 = Spooled (print) output file 4 = Diskette file 5 = Tape file 9 = Save file 10 = DDM file 11 = ICF file 20 = Inline data file 21 = Database file member
149	151	Char(3)	Reserved.
152	153	Bin(2)	Number of rows on the display for a WORKSTN device file.
154	155	Bin(2)	Number of columns on the display for a WORKSTN device file.
156	159	Bin(4)	**Number of records** in the file (member) when the member was opened. For joined database logical files, this value represents the number of records in the primary based-on physical file. When MBR(*ALL) is specified for an OVRDBF command, this value is updated as the first record of each member is read.
160	161	Char(2)	Type of file access for the DISK (database) device file. AR Arrival sequence KC Key sequence with duplicate keys allowed. Duplicate keys are processed in First-changed-first-out (FCFO) order. KF Key sequence with duplicate keys allowed. Duplicate keys are processed in First-in-first-out (FIFO) order. KL Key sequence with duplicate keys allowed. Duplicate keys are processed in Last-in-first-out (LIFO) order. KN Key sequence with duplicate keys allowed. Duplicate key processing sequence is not specified. KU Key sequence with unique key processing.
162	162	Char(1)	Duplicate key indication. Valid entries are as follows: D Duplicate keys are allowed. U Unique keys are required.

Positions From	To	Type (size)	Description
163	163	Char(1)	Source file member. 'Y' = this is a source file member; any other value indicates that this is not a source file.
164	173	Char(10)	User file control block.
174	183	Char(10)	User file control block overrides.
184	185	Bin(2)	Offset to volume ID labels (within this data structure). Valid for diskette and tape device files only.
186	187	Bin(2)	Maximum number of records that can be read or written as a block. For block I/O files only.
188	189	Bin(2)	Overflow line number for spooled (print) output files.
190	191	Bin(2)	Blocked record I/O record increment.
192	196	Char(5)	Reserved.
197	206	Char(10)	The named of the program device for ICF file, or the workstation device description ID for workstation display device files.
207	208	Bin(2)	Number of shared file opens. If the file is non-shared, this subfield will equal 1.
209	210	Bin(2)	Reserved.
211	212	Bin(2)	Number of based-on physical file members opened for a logical file. If the file being opened is a physical file member, this subfield will equal 1.

Positions From	To	Type (size)	Description
213	213	Char(1)	Device file flags. The 8 bits of this bytes are used to test for specific characteristics about the device file. The bit mask is as follows: Bit 1: Multiple Member Processing. 0 = A single member is being processed. 1 = *ALL members are being processed. Bit 2 Join Logical File Indicator 0 = File is not a join logical file. 1 = File is a join logical file. Bit 3 Local or Remote File 0 = File is on local system. 1 = File is on a remote system. Bit 4 Remote System Type (If Bit 3 = 1) 0 = File is on a remote AS/400 or System/38. 1 = File is on some other type of system. Bit 5 INDARA Keyword Used in DDS 0 = INDARA was not used in the DDS for the file. 1 = INDARA was used in the DDS for the file, and the indicators do not appear in the input buffer for the file. Bit 6 User Buffers 0 = The system creates I/O buffers for the file. 1 = The program supplies I/O buffers for the file. Bits 7 - 8 Reserved.
214	215	Char(2)	Unique Open Identifier. This value can be used to match I/O operations between this file and an associated data queue (*DTAQ). Each non-shared open, (including the first shared open) will have a unique ID. Subsequent RPG programs performing a shared open will have the same Open Identifier as other programs.
216	217	Bin(2)	Maximum length of a record for the file. This value includes hidden and parameter fields defined in WORKSTN device files.

Table 37: File Information Data Structure (INFDS)

Index

Index

UMONTH, 19
USROPN, 40
UYEAR, 19

—V—

Variable starting line number, 40

—W—

Workstation, 36
WORKSTN device, 34, 40
WRITE operation, 7

Index